Special Needs in the Early

This highly popular and accessible text contains a wealth of information about how early years staff can work effectively with professionals and parents to help identify and meet a range of special educational needs. This book aims to explore the most effective ways of supporting the child and implementing that support across the child's day-to-day life.

Now in its third edition, *Special Needs in the Early Years* is fully updated to reflect current policy, and topics covered include:

- early identification;
- effective communication with parents and carers;
- an exploration of the legal context;
- how to implement joint planning for identified needs;
- a consideration of the issues affecting collaboration.

With case studies, checklists, suggestions for good practice and cartoons to illustrate and enrich the text throughout, this book is structured to be easily accessible and invaluable for those who are in training to work in the early years sector. It will also be of interest to students on foundation courses and undergraduate students on early childhood education and childcare courses as well as more experienced practitioners.

Sue Roffey is adjunct Associate Professor at the University of Western Sydney, Honorary Lecturer at University College, London and international educational consultant. She is also the Founder and Director of Wellbeing Australia. She has previously authored *Helping with Behaviour in the Early Years: Promoting the positive and dealing with the difficult*, *School Behaviour and Families: Frameworks for working together* and *Young Children and Classroom Behaviour*.

John Parry is Lecturer in Education (Early Years and Inclusion) at the Open University. He has many years' experience as a practitioner working in the early years sector, primarily as a teacher and co-ordinator of a Portage service. From 2003 until 2009 he was Chairperson of the National Portage Association in the UK.

Special Needs in the Early Years

Supporting collaboration, communication and co-ordination

Third edition

Sue Roffey and John Parry

Routledge
Taylor & Francis Group

LONDON AND NEW YORK

Third edition published 2014
by Routledge
2 Park Square, Milton Park, Abingdon, Oxon OX14 4RN

and by Routledge
711 Third Avenue, New York, NY 10017

Routledge is an imprint of the Taylor & Francis Group, an informa business

© 2014 Sue Roffey and John Parry

First edition published by David Fulton Publishers 1999

Second edition published by David Fulton Publishers 2001

British Library Cataloguing in Publication Data
A catalogue record for this book is available from the British Library

Library of Congress Cataloging in Publication Data
A catalog record for this book has been requested

ISBN: 978-0-415-50475-1 (hbk)
ISBN: 978-0-415-50476-8 (pbk)
ISBN: 978-0-203-12802-2 (ebk)

Typeset in Sabon
by Wearset Ltd, Boldon, Tyne and Wear

Printed and bound in Great Britain by
TJ International Ltd, Padstow, Cornwall

This edition is dedicated to Mollie White, an inspirational educator of young children.

Contents

Preface

There have been some major developments in policy and guidance for special needs in the early years since the second edition of this book, and a welcome increase in emphasis on multi-disciplinary collaboration and the role of parents. There is also universal recognition about the importance of early intervention and how much difference this makes to optimal development for individual children. This is the case in all four principalities in the UK, although differences exist in the specifics of legislation as more powers are devolved to Scotland, Wales and Northern Ireland.

Early years practitioners need to know the formal frameworks within which they are working and therefore the expectations that are placed on them. This is covered in some detail in the first chapters of the book. Of equal importance, however, are the actual practices that enable these processes to take place smoothly and effectively. This is inseparable from a set of values about relationships and awareness of the interpersonal skills that actively demonstrate respect, understanding, empathy, inclusion and positivity. This is not just between parents and practitioners but also between diverse groups of professionals. The later chapters of the book are concerned with the promotion of optimal practices. It is these that are not subject to changes in legislation and are enduring across time and contexts.

This book is primarily written for early years practitioners, both in practice and in training – but is also intended to be a resource for all those working in this area. Our main focus is the promotion of effective communication and collaboration to ensure that a child's needs are met in early years settings, particularly in partnership with families. There is a focus on inclusive practices and the needs of teachers and pre-school practitioners in mainstream provision who may be less experienced in working with young children with special educational needs and their parents. This book is intended to be a resource that will:

- clarify the legal frameworks within which people are working;
- clarify the roles that different professionals may have;
- raise issues related to communication with parents;
- ensure that multi-disciplinary meetings are effective;
- provide a framework for joint planning;
- explore ways of strengthening in-school communication and collaboration between different settings and services;
- give examples of good practice which might be replicated or adapted; and
- provide easily accessible resource information.

This book covers the range and continuum of special educational needs, from those that are complex and require substantive intervention throughout a child's early years and education to those that are mild or temporary. Although 'early years' is defined in the Early Years Foundation Stage (EYFS) as between birth and five years, we have decided to maintain our focus on the Children Act definition, which is up to the age of eight and therefore through the first years of formal schooling.

The book is illustrated throughout by real-life experiences and also by some of the many examples of excellent practice that are now in place across the country.

Special note: the use of the pronouns 'he' and 'she' for children are used in alternate chapters, with the exception of Chapter 5 where this alternates throughout. The definition of 'parent' includes all those who have a legal or practical responsibility for the child's care and welfare. Where teachers are mentioned this also refers to any professional working within a pre-school setting or infant school. 'Pre-school settings' include all early years educational provision, including nurseries, Sure Start Children's Centres and playgroups.

Sue Roffey
John Parry
February 2013

Acknowledgements

We would like to acknowledge those who gave their time to talk to us for the case studies and examples of good practice throughout the book. It is heart-warming to see that despite the difficulties, there are many institutions and individuals committed to working with positive, evidence-based practice to promote the wellbeing of children, whatever their level of need.

We would like to thank Sonia Maskell and all at West Sussex Portage; Queenie McNally; Sally Harrison; Theresa Lane and all at Rachel McMillan Nursery and Children's Centre; Audrey Cooper; Joy Reynolds and all at Lanterns Nursery School and Children's Centre; Jenny Barclay; the Slingsby family; and Philip Peatfield.

We want to thank our families, especially John's partner Nik for her support, patience and durability and Sue's partner David for formatting the entire manuscript, checking references and being an overall good guy!

Thanks are again due to Nic Watts, who provided the illustrations, and to Emily Perl Kingsley for permission to reproduce 'Welcome to Holland'. Also thanks to Sue's daughter Emma Marshall for the cover photograph.

Chapter 1

Introduction

This book is about one of the most crucial factors in special education – the way people work together to achieve the best possible outcomes for the child.

Collaboration, verified by good communication and relational practices, facilitates a co-ordinated approach. This is of vital importance for all children but especially so in the early years, where it can make a significant difference to children, their families and those working with them. It is essential both to ensure clarity of aims and continuity of progress for the child and to promote confidence in parents and teachers in meeting children's needs. Good communication is about sharing aims, participation in decision making, planning, reviewing and making the best use of resources. It is also about reassurance.

Positive relationships require mutual respect, trust and a range of interpersonal skills. These qualities and abilities underpin *how* communication takes place. This has a significant impact on what is heard and ultimately what happens for each individual child. We are therefore concerned here about both the content and the process of communication, how information is shared taking account of contexts and especially the facilitation of partnership with parents.

Our focus here is on the whole range of special needs that children may have and how to best give all those individuals an educational experience that promotes their optimal wellbeing, learning and inclusion.

We provide case studies and examples of good practice throughout the text to both illustrate the issues involved and explore what needs to be taken into account to promote positive collaborative practices.

'It takes a village'

The much-quoted African proverb 'It takes a village to raise a child' is especially true when it comes to children with special educational needs (SEN). In Britain today, this 'village' is not only a group of neighbours or extended families but a whole community of professionals, advisors, teachers and others who support the family's efforts and help the child make optimum progress.

Sometimes a child's special needs are evident at or soon after birth. For many other families, the realisation that their child has a difficulty in one or more areas of development unravels more slowly. Whichever is the case, the child's needs become the focus for a number of adults who have a range of views, concerns and priorities. These individuals will come from some or all of the following groups:

- the parents and immediate family;
- extended family and close friends;
- others who will be caring for the child at home, nursery or pre-school provision;
- medical or paramedical professionals such as health visitors, doctors, speech therapists and physiotherapists;
- educational professionals such as teachers, pre-school co-ordinators, educational psychologists and specialist services such as Portage;
- social services personnel, which may include specialist social workers and those in respite schemes;
- other support services such as a Children's Centre outreach worker, independent parental support worker in a parent partnership scheme and keyworker;
- voluntary agencies;
- those responsible for the administration of special needs procedures in local authorities' Children's Services.

The child is part of a number of different systems in which she lives and learns. She is part of a family network, part of an education system and a direct user of the health services. She may also be a direct or indirect user of social services. These systems overlap and interact at given points and at certain times. Some individuals in these systems are close to the child and may be in contact on a daily basis. Others are more peripheral but nevertheless exert an influence on what happens for the child as they are linked in some way to the systems and the people who support the child's development. Bronfenbrenner (1979) has been highly influential in his ecological view of child development, saying that although the micro-system, which is what happens in the child's immediate environment, is most important, other systems such as local community facilities, workplace organisation and the socio-political culture all impact on outcomes for children.

When something happens in one system, there will be shifts elsewhere. Whether they realise it or not, the various people involved with the child, either directly or indirectly, affect what happens for the individual. A mother who feels supported may have more emotional energy to interact positively with her child, who may respond more readily, and may make more progress as a result. A family who have felt uncomfortable with one professional may be more wary of the next one they come into contact with and there will be barriers to communication that again may have consequences down the line. An early years worker who has fully understood what a physiotherapist has advised, and has felt able to clarify any uncertainties in a meeting, will be more skilled in adapting the environment appropriately for the child. A professional who feels under pressure and under-valued may be highly stressed and consequently lack sensitivity and patience with clients. The expectations and influence of a member of the extended family may influence how a parent sees his child, and this in turn affects how he perceives the advice given to him. How disability is portrayed in the wider culture makes a difference to how ordinary people respond to the disabled.

Roles and responsibilities

Although all professionals would say they want the best for the child in question, each has their own perspectives and priorities. They all have different roles and

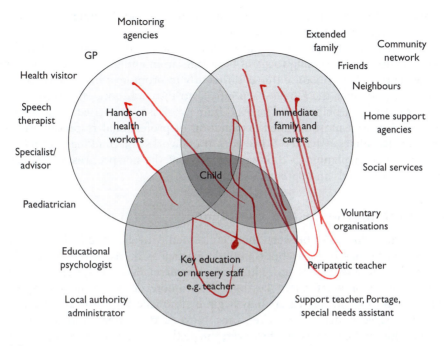

Monitoring agencies

GP

Health visitor

Speech therapist

Specialist/ advisor

Paediatrician

Educational psychologist

Local authority administrator

Hands-on health workers

Child

Key education or nursery staff e.g. teacher

Extended family

Friends

Community network

Neighbours

Immediate family and carers

Home support agencies

Social services

Voluntary organisations

Peripatetic teacher

Support teacher, Portage, special needs assistant

Figure 1.1

responsibilities and are operating within different contexts. Some are involved in order to make a particular kind of assessment and offer advice, others to work with the child to promote development; some will be more concerned with monitoring progress, others with supporting the family. Some, especially teachers, will see the child as one of many; for her parents she is the priority – but also part of the wider family. Some of these roles are multiple, others overlap and sometimes it may not be entirely clear who is supposed to be doing what.

It takes a determined effort to develop this potentially disparate and fragmented group of individuals into a cooperative team who are able to communicate effectively with each other to meet the needs of the whole child within the context of her whole family and in a whole class group. The fact that traditionally professionals come from different disciplines, which have different organisational structures and different funding arrangements, has not helped. In many places, geographical boundaries are not in alignment and there is a need to work across these. People may not know about the context in which other colleagues are working, and even the definitions used may be different. Some people, particularly in the health services, may see the child as having an innate problem that requires 'treatment', whereas professionals in education and social services usually have a more interactive perspective.

Although interdisciplinary practice is a much-valued concept, and increasingly seen in the legislation, the reality is plagued with difficulties and differs across contexts. Many parents have found themselves in the position of passing information around, sometimes at a time when they may themselves feel confused and unclear.

Sometimes their confusion has been exacerbated by the different things they hear from the range of professionals they meet.

There is no doubt, however, that from the last decade of the twentieth century, there has been an increasing focus in both legislation and guidance across all principalities in the UK to organise things differently to promote a higher level of collaboration. In particular there have been efforts to respond more effectively to parents and foster their participation. The legal framework is summarised in Chapter 2, and Chapter 3 gives a more detailed explanation of professional responsibilities within different disciplines. Chapter 5 provides frameworks for thinking through what is involved in joint planning – taking into account the perspectives and strengths of diverse professionals and parents.

Levels of knowledge and confidence

An important difference between those concerned with the child is the type and level of knowledge they possess about a child's particular needs, about the child within the family and about SEN procedures and resources. Knowledge gives rise both to confidence about what might be done to promote development and appropriate expectations. Parents and carers may begin by knowing very little about their child's particular special needs, but over time may become more knowledgeable than anyone else. In the early years, however, the plethora of advice and suggestions from many different concerned sources may only add to the feelings of anxiety, frustration, guilt and confusion that often beset a family who are learning to come to terms with, adjust to and manage their child's special needs. Chapter 4 details some of the issues that need to be taken into account in those early days when children's needs are first identified.

With an increased focus on providing a mainstream experience for most children with SEN, and including them in many of the activities and experiences that are open to others of the same age, more adults in early years settings are coming into contact with and supporting children who have a range of needs. In the same way that parents may be more or less knowledgeable and confident, this is also true for early years professionals. Where people are clearer about what is expected of them, and feel that they have the resources or support to do what might be required, it is easier for them to welcome children and their families warmly and positively.

With the family's agreement, it is helpful if knowledge is shared about the whole child and the contexts in which she both lives and learns. A chance remark or suggestion which shows little understanding about demands on the family or special needs procedures can serve to increase guilt or raise unrealistic expectations that may generate frustration and conflict.

Development, progress and change

Any child's needs and development do not remain static and, especially in the early years, can change considerably over a few months. Good communication enhances continuity, especially during transition periods and when new people become involved. Chapter 6 is concerned with aspects of communication and liaison within an early years setting and school. It also looks at what needs to happen when children move on. Good, regular, liaison ensures there will be a consistency of approach, evaluation of intervention, updated programmes, and that any new information is shared and taken into account when planning.

As some children identified with SEN may learn and progress in ways people are not used to, it is important that people hold onto the progress that children are in fact making, even if this is in the smallest of steps. It is worthwhile to reflect sometimes on progress made over longer periods so that everyone can be reminded of the results of their efforts. The review process for children with special educational needs is supposed to do this but it sometimes gets lost in the enthusiasm to plan forward.

Chapter 7 explores the issues affecting collaboration – both those that promote and foster good practice and those that are likely to inhibit it. Time is critical in education. Among other things, this chapter looks at how to use the finite resource most effectively.

The importance of early intervention

All current legislation and guidance on children's special educational needs puts a firm emphasis on the importance of early intervention. There are some obvious reasons for this and others which are more subtle but equally important.

Promoting development

The more obvious reason for early intervention is that the earlier a child's needs are addressed and, where appropriate, programmes put into place, then the more progress the child is likely to make. Babies and small children are at their most adaptable and flexible, and their brains more able to take on board new ways of working. The younger a child is when intervention begins, the more chance there will be of making optimum progress – so long as the programme devised is appropriate for her developmental stage and suitable for her learning needs and compatible with her family context.

It is critical that the child is seen as a whole person and each area of their development is given attention. Where the child's difficulties and their remediation are the overwhelming focus for the entire family there is a danger that normal elements of functioning are ignored, possibly with negative consequences for the child's well-being in other areas. Collaboration and communication between parents, teachers and professionals will not only help to identify intervention but also ensure that the child's needs are seen in the context of her overall development.

Maintaining the child's positive sense of self

Self-concept is not necessarily the first thing people think of when considering the importance of early intervention. When a child has inappropriate demands made on her, however, and experiences failure on a regular basis she may develop a view of herself as someone who 'can't' or 'is lazy' or who causes her parents distress. The child who experiences continual failure will eventually be reluctant to try and this will impede her progress even further. The earlier there is a good understanding of the child's difficulties and needs, the earlier there will be appropriate expectations and celebration of success when these are achieved. At the opposite end of the spectrum some parents are so protective of their child they do everything for her. These expectations are equally inappropriate and do not encourage the child to try things for herself and develop optimum independence.

Supporting parents

Emotional support

Much has been written about working in partnership, but it is in these early days when a child's SEN are first identified that the interactions between the family and others are at their most crucial. The experience of having to face the reality that your child may in some way be seen as different from others is potentially devastating. There is evidence to indicate that the circumstances surrounding this initial awareness have an impact on levels of coping skills and depression later on (Baird *et al.*, 2000).

Many families go through what is often described as a period of grief. As with bereavement, parents may go through stages of denial, shock, anger, guilt, overwhelming sadness and sometimes depression before they are able to accept the reality of their child's special needs. For some families that point never really comes. The professionals who come into contact with parents, especially in the early days, may face some of these emotional responses and need to be prepared for them. Initial approaches to parents make a difference to how they view the professionals they will meet in the future. What is said to parents at this time also impinges on their feelings about themselves and their child. These include feelings of guilt that so often accompany having a child with difficulties, their anxieties about the future for their child and how she will manage and the future for themselves and how they will cope. There are also likely to be concerns about effects on the rest of the family. Having a child with disability or other special needs is challenging on all family relationships – single-parent status climbs markedly in the first years of a child's life, for instance (Clarke and McKay, 2008). These additional and related stressors need to be acknowledged and taken into account.

Finding the right balance between acknowledgement of the parents' emotional response, the reality of the situation and being positive about the possibilities is not easy. Consideration needs to be given to the way information is delivered, the timing of this, the amount of information to give and the support parents need.

The strength of the support network for carers will be linked to the progress the child makes. Parents who can go to others who will listen, accept their child, not be judgmental and offer advice and guidance when it is asked for may be better able to come to terms with what has happened and forge a more positive relationship with their child. Often this support network includes the professionals with whom the parent comes into contact, as well as the extended family, voluntary groups and other families. In some cases, it may be the entire support network the parent has.

It is important to remember that parents often have many other demands on them. The child who is the focus for the professionals is only one of a family's concerns and parents may worry about the effects on their other children. Working 'with' parents means being able to take into consideration not only what it is

Welcome to Holland

by Emily Perl Kingsley

'I am often asked to describe the experience of raising a child with a disability – to try to help people who have not shared that unique experience to understand it, to imagine how it would feel. It's like this ...

'When you are going to have a baby, it's like planning a fabulous vacation trip – to Italy. You buy a bunch of guidebooks and make your wonderful plans. The Coliseum. The Michelangelo David. The gondolas in Venice. You may learn some handy phrases in Italian. It's all very exciting.

'After months of eager anticipation, the day finally arrives. You pack your bags and off you go. Several hours later, the plane lands. The stewardess comes in and says, "Welcome to Holland."

'"Holland?!?" you say. "What do you mean Holland?? I signed up for Italy! I'm supposed to be in Italy. All my life I've dreamed of going to Italy." But there's been a change in the flight plan. They've landed in Holland and there you must stay.

'The important thing is that they haven't taken you to a horrible, disgusting, filthy place, full of pestilence, famine and disease. It's just a different place.

'So you must go out and buy new guidebooks. And you must learn a whole new language. And you will meet a whole new group of people you would never have met.

'It's just a different place. It's slower paced than Italy, less flashy than Italy. But after you've been there for a while and you catch your breath, you look around ... and you begin to notice that Holland has windmills ... and Holland has tulips. Holland even has Rembrandts.

'But everyone you know is busy coming and going from Italy ... and they're all bragging about what a great time they had there. And for the rest of your life, you will say "Yes, that's where I was supposed to go. That's what I had planned".

'And the pain of that will never, ever, ever, ever go away ... because the loss of that dream is a very very significant loss.

'But ... if you spend your life mourning the fact that you didn't get to Italy, you may never be free to enjoy the very special, the very lovely things ... about Holland.'

Figure 1.2 'Welcome to Holland' by Emily Perl Kingsley.

possible for them to do but also what is feasible. Unless parents are truly part of the decision-making process they may agree to something that is, in effect, unrealistic. This may only serve to increase the guilt they may already be feeling and put further demands on an already over-stretched family.

The vivid analogy in Figure 1.2 was given by a parent to illustrate how it felt for her to have to come to terms with having a child with complex special needs.

Information support

As can be seen from the above, it can not only be distressing emotionally in these early days following identification, it can also be highly confusing. Professionals who spend their working lives in the SEN world may not fully realise that the structures, language and understandings which are so familiar to them on a daily basis are often completely foreign to others. Parents need to be able to ask the same things over and over again and it may be helpful if information comes from a variety of sources, including, and perhaps especially, other families who have had similar experiences. Written guidance that parents can refer to in their own time is also useful.

When a child's SEN are first identified parents may want the answers to questions that are difficult, if not impossible, to answer with any level of precision. They may want professionals to predict specific or long-term outcomes for their child or they may want to know exactly what support will be available. Sometimes professionals are reluctant to say that they do not know the answer to something for fear this may damage their credibility. It is, however, better to outline the range of possibilities, or the processes by which decisions will be made, than to give what appear to be concrete and substantive facts which are actually ill-informed, potentially misleading and raise inappropriate expectations. It may be tempting to tell parents what they would like to hear to alleviate their distress, but this only leads to greater grief later on and may damage relationships with other professionals. It is also not helpful to outline all the potential difficulties at the outset as this may raise anxiety unnecessarily.

Professionals need to take their lead from parents: although too much detailed information at once may not be helpful, parents should be given information as to how to access what they need to know and feel comfortable about asking. The last thing parents need at this time is to feel they are being kept in the dark in any way or denied information that may be useful, however well-intentioned this might be. Even though they cannot be given definitive answers to everything, parents need good, accessible information in a language they can understand. This includes both their home language and explanation of any acronyms or specialised terminology. Words and acronyms that are used daily by professionals may be meaningless to families and many people are reluctant to say they don't understand.

Information could include some or all of the following, depending on the special needs identified, the level and complexity of these, and who is most involved at this early stage:

- reassurance that parents are an essential part of any decision making and intervention;

- discussion of any immediate action that it is appropriate and agreed to take on behalf of the child and the rationale for this: e.g. observation over a given period, programme to develop certain skills, any referrals, etc.;
- names and contact details of the local Children's Centre and Parent Partnership Scheme;
- information about the early support or key-working service who will be the main contacts for the family and the arrangements for communicating with these people;
- details of any local support groups;
- names and contact details of any relevant voluntary organisation;
- if the child is in a pre-school setting, a copy of the SEN and inclusion policy;
- information about policies relating to target setting and individual education plans (IEPs) such as Early Years Action and Action Plus procedures;
- the range of provision available and criteria for accessing that provision;
- review arrangements;
- information about the 'local offer' for families clarifying what support they should receive and from whom within a local authority.

Case study: Supporting vulnerable children – an extension of the Portage Service in York

Since 2004 the York Portage Service has extended its remit from working with pre-school children with disabilities and SEN and their families to Sure Start Portage, which includes two other groups of vulnerable children:

1. children who are low birth weight and pre-term;
2. pre-school children who are 'looked after'.

Initially the extension of the service was made possible by drawing on additional funds from the Sure Start Programme, but it has now been core funded and made available throughout the city. The same model of service delivery is provided for children in these groups as for those referred to the main Portage service. Each family is visited by their Portage home visitor for weekly visits that last around an hour. At each visit, play and learning activities are planned by the home visitor and parent/carer working together. These will then be carried out at home before the next visit. The activities may be small steps towards a developmental goal for the child, such as grasping a toy or sitting unaided. They may also represent more general ideas for play, stimulation and developing communication.

When Sure Start Portage was set up it was planned that the support would be for six months, but if there is a need for a longer period of support then the service may provide further home visits. This can be particularly appropriate for children who are born pre-term or with low birth weight as their early lives are often disrupted by frequent hospital admissions and appointments. Sometimes children will be referred to the main Portage service at the end of the initial six-month period if it has become evident that their additional support needs are significant and likely to be more long term.

Children who are low birth weight or pre-term are often referred to the service via the paediatric team, for example the Special Care Baby Unit Outreach Sister or Paediatrician. As a result, support can begin close to the time that the child returns home from hospital. Other sources of referral have been health visitors, Children's Centre workers, the Early Support Keyworker Co-ordinators and parents themselves.

Feedback from parents through exit questionnaires has been overwhelmingly positive. One mother who was referred because her baby was pre-term felt that the home visits had alleviated her early concerns over her child's general development. Following just over six months of support it was agreed by the family and service that regular Portage was no longer necessary. In the same week the parents were told that they no longer needed to see the paediatric team because there were no outstanding concerns. The changes were relayed to the family's health visitor and ongoing support was organised through the local Children's Centre and toddler playgroup.

It is a statutory requirement that all children who become 'looked after' have an initial health assessment, including consideration of physical health, emotional and mental health, wellbeing and health promotion. In York, for pre-school children, one outcome of this assessment can be a referral by the paediatrician and social worker to the Portage service. The focus of the home visits for this group are on providing general advice on play and early stimulation. Visits are usually to foster carers, although the child's parents can also be involved if they have contact time or if there is a programme in place to re-unite the family. As part of transition support from foster care to adoption, the Portage team may also contribute to a video story and a 'This is me' booklet about the child in order to help introduce the child to their adoptive parents.

Both of these aspects of the Portage service's work are overseen by a multi-agency steering group drawn from the wide range of professionals involved. Therefore, at all levels the projects require a commitment to integrated working in order to offer the optimum support to vulnerable children. Such additions to the standard Portage provision also serve as a reminder that supporting children with special needs in the early years requires taking a broad perspective on who may require additional support.

Chapter 2

The legal context

The people who work on behalf of young disabled children and children with SEN do so within a complex framework of legislation and guidance. Although everyone must take note of all legislation, the emphasis for them may depend on their particular profession and who employs them. However, in recent years guidance and legislation has focused on developing joined-up services in order to improve outcomes for all children. Consequently the policy framework underpinning early years work has become much more integrated and less specific to health, education or social care sectors. Additionally, the legal and policy context framing the work of practitioners who support young children with SEN has to be viewed on two levels: the overarching guidance that applies to all young children; and the specific legislation covering the provision for young people with additional requirements.

A further complication in considering the legislative framework in the sector has been the gradual devolution of power to the Scottish, Welsh and Northern Ireland Assemblies. This has resulted in variations in policies between the four principalities that has also influenced practice and how settings operate around the UK. Table 2.1 provides some idea of both the overarching and specific legislative frameworks that developed in the four home nations over the period since 2000.

This brief summary highlights the complexity of the legislation and policy surrounding services and support for children with SEN. Probably the framework you are working with at the time of reading this book has shifted from this outline because the educational provision for young children is often at the forefront of political debate and likely to be adjusted with each change of government or administration. However, looking back at legislation and guidance from the 1990s onwards, it is evident that certain themes have emerged which are central to the response to children with SEN and their families and likely to influence the requirements and expectations made of practitioners well into the future.

Themes of legislation, guidance and policy

Promoting children's rights and anti-discrimination

It is important to realise that developments in international law have been a major influence on early years legislation and policy in Britain in recent years. The United Nations Convention on the Rights of the Child (UNCRC) was adopted by the United Nations in November 1989 and was ratified by the UK in 1991. The

Table 2.1 Key legislation and policies in the UK

England: overarching legislation and policies
Sure Start Programme (1999) – Providing additional quality services to young children and their families in areas identified as experiencing high levels of deprivation.

'Every Child Matters' (2003) – Focused on the structure of services to achieve fundamental outcomes: being healthy; staying safe; enjoying and achieving; making a positive contribution; and economic well-being.

The Children Act (2004) – Required local authorities in England to re-organise their services. Education and Social Services Departments were amalgamated into Children's Services.

The Childcare Act (2006) – Required local authorities to make specific provision in the early years sector. Defined a 'young child' as a child aged between birth and the end of the August following their fifth birthday.

Supporting Families in the Foundation Years (2011) – This joint departmental policy document set out the incoming government's aspirations for the sector and for supporting young children and their families.

The Early Years Foundation Stage (EYFS) (2012) – This sets the standards for the learning, development and care of children from birth to five. As well as providing the framework for an early years curriculum, the EYFS also requires settings to review children's progress at two years old and provide a written summary for parents and carers.

England: specific legislation and policies
The Education Act (1993 and 1996) – The Education Act 1993 required local authorities to assess and make provision for children with SEN. The 1996 Act established that a Code of Practice should be followed to ensure consistency and quality of assessments of SEN.

SEN code of Practice (2001) – All local authorities, schools and early years settings were required to work within the Code, which set out a graduated process of assessment.

The Special Educational Needs (SEN) and Disability Act (2001) – This strengthened the right of children with SEN to be educated in mainstream settings and applied the duties laid down in the 1995 Disability Discrimination legislation to education settings.

Support and Aspiration: A new approach to Special Educational Needs and Disability (2011) – This proposed simplifying the formal assessment process and a more robust system for identifying SEN in the early years involving health professionals and early years practitioners.

Children and Families Bill (2013) – Part 3 of this bill put forward legislation to amend the 1996 Education Act, replacing statements with Education and Health Care plans. The new Act also required each local authority to publish a 'local offer' of the provision available for children and young people identified with SEN.

Scotland: overarching legislation and policies
Getting it Right for Every Child (2006) – This set out the outcomes essential to children developing as successful learners, confident individuals, effective contributors and responsible citizens. The aim was for children to be: safe, nurtured, able to achieve; healthy; active; respected; responsible; and included.

Early Years Framework (2008) – This shifted the focus of service planning, design and delivery away from crisis management towards prevention, early identification and early intervention by universal agencies.

The Curriculum for Excellence (2010) – This established the curriculum for all children aged 3–18 years to enable all learners to be challenged and reach their full potential.

(continued)

Scotland: specific legislation and policies
The Education (Additional Support for Learning) Act (2004 and 2009) – This set out how children with additional support needs should be provided for by local authorities, supported, as necessary, by appropriate agencies.

Supporting Children's Learning Code of Practice (2010) – All local authorities, schools and early years settings were required to work within the Code, which set the process of assessment of additional support needs. It detailed the requirements for single agency plans; statutory Co-ordinated Support Plans were added to the guidance.

Wales: overarching legislation and policies
Flying Start (2005) – This focused on developing services for children and families in specified catchment areas around infant and primary schools and providing free part-time childcare for two-year-olds and enhanced family services.

The Foundation Phase (2008) – The curriculum planned as a progressive framework that spanned four years (3–7 years of age) to meet the diverse needs of all children, including those who are at an earlier stage of development and those who are more able.

Wales: specific legislation and policies
SEN Code of Practice (2002) – This detailed the statutory duties towards children with SEN in schools and early years settings. The Code was designed to help provision to make effective decisions rather than dictate responses. This was similar to the Code of Practice in England.

Northern Ireland: overarching legislation and policies
Pre-school Expansion Programme (1998) – This aimed to provide a pre-school place to every child for at least a year before starting school. By 2005, 92 per cent of children received such provision.

Curricular Guidance for Pre-school Education (2005) – This gave non-statutory guidance on providing for the learning experience of all children. The statutory curriculum begins in Year 1 of primary.

Northern Ireland: specific legislation and policies
Education (Northern Ireland) Order (1996)/Special Educational Needs (Northern Ireland) Order (2005) – This set out the staged assessment process and strengthened the expectation of inclusion in mainstream settings. Early years providers were not formally required to apply the Code.

Every School a good school: Review of Special Educational Needs and Inclusion (2012) – This set out proposed changes to the Code of Practice and legislation to be in place by 2014. The staged assessment process was to be simplified and the Code of Practice extended to cover the pre-school sector.

Convention represented 'an internationally agreed framework of minimum standards necessary for the well-being of the child, to which every child and young person under 18 is entitled' (DENI, 2010, p. 10). As a signatory the UK has committed to make legislative changes and to designate government funding in order to maintain these minimum standards for young people. Articles 28 and 29 covered the right to education provided on 'the basis of equal opportunity' and with a view to prepare children for 'responsible life in a free society'. Article 23 of the Convention stated the rights of disabled children to experience a 'full and decent life' and 'active participation in the community'. In addition this Article underlined that the focus of education should be to achieve 'the fullest possible social integration' (Office of the High Commissioner for Human Rights, 2011).

Running alongside international human rights legislation that informs our domestic early years policy, there has been significant emphasis on the development of robust anti-discrimination laws in Britain. This culminated with the 2010 Equality Act covering the whole of the UK and drawing together all the previous legislation around equality and discrimination – for example the 2005 Disability Discrimination Act and the 2006 Equality Bill. The Act made it unlawful to discriminate on the grounds of sex, race, disability, gender, sexual orientation, and religion or belief when providing services. So, for example, an early years setting could not refuse to provide or restrict the services they offered on the basis of a child's disability.

It seems likely that the development of children's rights and social justice will continue to underpin progressive policy and legislation affecting children and families, because governments and communities recognise that: 'out of it will emerge a better world for children and this will rebound to the benefit not only of children but of all of us' (Freeman, 2007, p. 20).

Early intervention and support

Policy makers have, over the years, increasingly made the connection between intervening as early as possible to support young children and families and the all-round long-term benefits for the wider community (HM Government, 2011). Such awareness of the importance of early support has motivated governments to generally increase access to pre-school education for all children. For example, in England by 2011 all three and four year olds were entitled to free sessions with a registered provider for up to 15 hours per week. There was also a government commitment to offer free provision to 'the most disadvantaged' two year olds by 2014, extending the entitlement to cover 40 per cent of this age group. In Wales, Scotland and Northern Ireland similar policies spreading the availability of free pre-school places to increasing numbers of children suggests the trend of establishing early childhood provision as part of the basic education system is a central theme of legislation.

As well as the general development of early education, long-term interventions like the Sure Start programme highlighted the trend in policy to target resources early for children and families who are likely to encounter disadvantage. In 1999 the government in England launched Sure Start in areas of high deprivation. This was designed to provide better service co-ordination, support and guidance to vulnerable families with babies and very young children. Sure Start local programmes were extended by progressive waves of funding and over time developed into an extensive network of Children's Centres in every ward in England (some 3,500 in total). By 2011 the new coalition government had committed to 'a new core purpose for Children's Centres, with early intervention at its heart' (DfE/DoH, 2011, p. 5), but were again aiming to focus this type of support on the most deprived areas of the country.

Although Sure Start began as an initiative in England, the devolved administrations in Scotland, Wales and Northern Ireland soon committed considerable funding to this model of early intervention. By 2010 there were 32 Sure Start Partnerships in Northern Ireland, and in Wales a programme called 'Flying Start' was funded from 2005 to set up similar support based in new Children's Centres or within local schools to serve specific catchment areas. Scotland also initially allocated Sure Start funding to all 32 of its local authorities, but by 2008 the 'Early Years Framework' was shifting attention to developing universal rather than targeted services. As part of this shift, the intention was announced to inspect all daycare provision on the standard of their early intervention work.

In addition to being a theme of general policy, early intervention has also been a particular focus of the legal and policy framework for the provision for disabled children and children with SEN. This is because policy makers recognise that:

> Through effective early identification and intervention – working with parents and families – we can reduce the impact that SEN or disability may have in the long run, and enable more young people to lead successful and independent adult lives.
>
> (DfE, 2011a, p. 29)

In England the Early Support programme has, since 2003, developed within the climate established by the Every Child Matters Agenda. It specifically looked at meeting the need for a joined-up approach to intervention for families with very young disabled children. By 2007 the implementation plan for Early Support throughout England was announced in the government policy document *Aiming High for Disabled Children: Better Support for Families* (DCSF/DoH, 2007). All local authorities were required to develop Early Support services which involved: providing a keyworker to co-ordinate the agencies working with individual families; allowing parents to be central to service planning for their own children; the introduction of family-held records and a Family Service plan; and the use of developmental journals which encouraged parents and professionals to assess children's progress together. By 2011 the English government were proposing that voluntary and community sector organisations should also be involved in developing the Early Support model, especially key working with families and children (DfE, 2011a). The importance of early years settings being part of the Early Support process through shared use of the materials and contributing to family plans was also highlighted in guidance for providers (NCB/DfE, 2012).

Initiatives such as Sure Start and Early Support show that the legislative and policy context affecting children with SEN has consistently developed around the theme of identifying and providing support as early as possible. This is a theme that long-term government policy has seemed determined to strengthen. From 2012, for example, providers in England have been required to carry out a progress check of all children in their setting around the age of two under the revised Early Years Foundation Stage (EYFS). This check focuses on the three prime areas of learning, as defined in the EYFS: communication and language; personal, social and emotional development; and physical development. Provided as a written summary for families, it is intended to link with the 'Healthy Child Review' carried out by health visitors at around the same time. The aim is to support parents' understanding of their child's needs through these checks and to enhance their ability to support development at home (NCB/DfE, 2012). From a central government perspective there was also an interest in raising general attainment by ensuring children were provided with additional support before entry to school. Similar commitment to developing proactive services has been shown in Scotland. Here the Assembly announced that by 2013 a new Children's Services Bill would be in place which would confirm a major shift towards services for all young people being based on: prevention; child-centred delivery; support for parents; and early intervention.

Interactive and continuous assessment (Codes of Practice)

A further theme of legislation and policy focusing on the support of young children with SEN has been to provide guidance around the nature of assessment. Significantly, a framework of assessment has developed that moves away from identifying a child's difficulties and deficits to consider strengths, personality and environmental factors that also have an impact. The intention has been to develop assessment procedures that enable parents, the child and the range of professionals working with them to put together a support programme. The emphasis has not been so much on what the child should do as on what should happen in order for him to make progress. The framework for good practice in assessment has therefore aimed to establish: appropriate expectations, adaptations, activities, responsibilities and approaches; as systems for inter-agency and home–school communication; and procedures for monitoring and review.

All four countries in the UK developed a Code of Practice to ensure consistent and effective response when assessing children's SEN. In England and Wales a revised Code was operational from 2002, and all early years settings were required to follow the guidance. All providers had to have clear policies for identifying, supporting and responding to children with SEN. They also needed to appoint a member of staff (a special needs co-ordinator) familiar with the Code of Practice and able to support other staff and parents with the assessment and provision process.

The assessment process represented a step-by-step or staged approach to observing and providing support for individual children. This consisted of three levels:

- *Early action*: where an initial concern was identified, support provided from within the group and the response to such support reviewed over time. An Individual Education Plan (IEP) was written to record the strategies used to support the child and several short-term learning targets for the child to work towards.
- *Early action plus*: where external support was involved to help the providers meet the child's educational requirements, for example specialised advice or support for specific activities. The move to the early action plus level followed a review within the setting of the IEP and the impact of strategies planned at the early action stage.
- *Statutory assessment*: where cause for significant concern continued despite the input at the early action plus stage, parents and settings could request a statutory assessment from the local authority (LA). In deciding whether to initiate a statutory assessment the LA would seek evidence about action already taken, how long intervention had been in place and views from parents and professionals most closely involved with the child and family. The outcome of a statutory assessment could be a statement of SEN, which was a legal document that detailed the framework of a learning programme and the extra resources that the LA must provide for the child.

In 2011 the coalition government in England proposed a major overhaul of the legis-lation and Code of Practice regarding the assessment of SEN.

A commitment was made to introduce by 2014 a new single assessment process that would lead to an 'Education, Health and Care Plan' (EHC), so replacing the 'Statement of Special Educational Needs'. This plan would be developed by all the services involved with the families, including the early years setting, and detail the support that would be provided for the child and family from all sectors, educa-tion, health and social care. The plan would be regularly reviewed and as a legal document commit all parties to provide the designated services. The overall aim was to develop a process which responded to 'the family's needs and ambitions for the child or young person's future outcomes covering education, health, employment and independence' (DfE, 2012a, p. 12).

Alongside these reforms there were plans to replace the categories in the SEN Code of practice with a single category of Special Educational Needs. The Code of Practice was to be revised to provide clear guidance on identifying children with SEN under this single category while ensuring 'a focus on outcomes rather than processes' (DfE, 2012a, p. 45). Some commentators took the view that the abandon-ment of the early action/early action plus categories meant that the SEN label would become applicable to a much narrower group of children and that some young people's needs would be missed. Others felt that the focus on a single category would concentrate provision justifiably on those with greatest need. For practition-ers, the importance of recognising the real children beneath the labels would always remain a priority, no matter what identification system was in place.

In Northern Ireland a Code of Practice has been operational since 1998, with some revisions taking place in 2005. Although the Code required the same general responses, the graduated assessment process was described in five stages:

Stage 1   The setting identifying and registering a child's SEN and consulting the SEN co-ordinator.
Stage 2   The SEN co-ordinator taking lead responsibility for collecting and recording information and for co-ordinating the child's special educational provision.
Stage 3   The practitioners and the SEN co-ordinator being supported by spe-cialists from outside the setting.
Stages 4 and 5 The Education Board assessing the need for and then if necessary issuing a Statement of Special Educational Needs.

In a review of Special Educational Needs and Inclusion in the Province in 2012, one of the proposed changes was to reduce the number of stages to three: school lead assessment and support; school lead assessment with external support from other agencies; and school provision enhanced by a 'Co-ordinated Support Plan'. This plan would be more multi-agency focused and intended to replace statements.

Pre-school settings in the province had broadly followed the stages within the Code but without being formally required to do so through legislation (DENI, 2005). By 2012 there were proposals as part of a wide-ranging review of SEN to require non-statutory voluntary and community settings that received government funding to have full regard to the Code of Practice (DENI, 2012).

In Scotland a different interpretation for the assessment of SEN has developed in legislation and guidance. The Education (Additional Support for Learning) Act 2004 and 2009 set out how children with additional support needs should be provided for by local authorities and supported, as necessary, by the appropriate agencies. The Scottish government's approach was in line with their *Getting it Right for Every Child* agenda and focused on agencies working together to meet individual children's needs. Importantly, the definition of additional support needs was broader than SEN, including, for example, children who were bullied or who were young carers. Therefore the overall guidance and Code of Practice was seen to apply to 'children or young people who, for whatever reason, require additional support, long or short term, in order to help them make the most of their school education' (Scottish Government, 2009, p. 5).

The Additional Support for Learning Acts state that in the early years, education authorities carry the duty to provide additional support for children over three and also for some younger children with recognised disabilities. Additional support could come from outside agencies – for example, speech and language therapy – as well as in the setting. The Acts and accompanying Code of Practice published in 2010 indicate that a staged approach to assessment should be used in much the same way as in England, Wales and Northern Ireland. Three stages of progressive assessment and provision were stipulated in the guidance:

Stage 1   Support and planning can be provided in existing provision. A single agency plan would be drawn up in the setting.
Stage 2   Support and planning to involve education specialists from outside the setting. An IEP would be put in place.
Stage 3   Support and planning to involve a wide range of agencies from outside the setting. A lead professional would co-ordinate a multi-agency plan for the child.

Finally, it was recognised that some children whose learning was likely to be shaped by complex long-term factors, would need a co-ordinated support plan in place of their multi-agency plan. This statutory document detailed: learning objectives; support required; who was responsible for providing the support; and where the child should receive such support. Children below pre-school age (defined as three years old) were not eligible for a co-ordinated support plan, but the other stages of assessment and planning could apply.

Inclusion

The process of 'integration' of children with SEN into mainstream settings was a common theme of guidance and legislation throughout the 1980s and early 1990s, which signified the belief that education for those with learning difficulties alongside their peers was good practice. However, such integration was proposed with limitations because it was only regarded as practicable for those children who could respond and adapt positively to mainstream provision, otherwise specialised education placements were required. Since the 1996 Education Act and the 2001 Special Educational Needs (SEN) and Disability Act the right of children with SEN to be educated in a mainstream setting has been strengthened and the concept of integration has developed into a philosophy of inclusion. The idea of inclusion implies the young person being part of something rather than additional to it, and takes account of all children rather than a few. The focus is on provision changing in order to accommodate all children rather than children having to meet certain developmental or behavioural criteria in order to attend. Fundamentally, inclusion is concerned with 'increasing the participation of children and young people in, and reducing their exclusion from, the cultures, activities and communities of local settings' (Booth and Ainscow, 2004, p. 4). Therefore, one of the major themes of legislation and guidance over the last two decades has been the increased focus on the development of inclusive practices to provide for the diversity of children's educational needs in the mainstream.

For school-aged children with SEN, however, the possibility of being included in mainstream school is not unconditional. Legislation in all four home nations has accommodated placement in a special school if the young person is assessed as adversely affecting other children's education in the mainstream setting or their parents wish them to attend specialised provision appropriate to their educational needs. If you look back at the section on children's rights and discrimination, you will realise that there seems to be a contradiction between the ideals of the UN convention and the actual practices of the British administrations.

Significantly, in 2009 the UK government refused to ratify all of the United Nations Convention on the Rights of Persons with Disabilities, exempting itself from Article 24, which considered education rights. This Article required states to act to 'ensure an inclusive education system at all levels' for disabled children and access to 'an inclusive, quality and free primary education and secondary education on an equal basis with others in the communities in which they live' (Article 24 UNCRPD, cited in CSIE, 2011). This suggests that in the UK the reservations about embarking on a policy course that would commit schools to the inclusive developments are likely to continue and the focus will be to 'strengthen parental choice by improving the range and diversity of schools from which parents can choose' (DfE, 2011a, p. 17).

Within the early years sector the promotion of inclusive practice and policy has generally seemed to be more readily accommodated. As you read in the section on children's rights, the 2010 Equalities Bill clearly placed expectations on early years settings as service providers to include young disabled children and make reasonable adjustments in order to accommodate all their users. In addition to such legal requirements, there seems to have been a general acceptance within curriculum guidance that inclusive practice is a fundamental characteristic of early years provision. For example, the EYFS introduced in England from 2012 is clear that:

> Providers must have and implement a policy, and procedures, to promote the equality of opportunity of children in their care ... [which covers] how the individual needs of all children will be met (including how those children who are disabled or who have special educational needs will be included, valued and supported, and how reasonable adjustments will be made for them).
>
> (DfE, 2012b, p. 26)

Similarly, the Foundation Phase document for Wales has provided clear guidance that:

> settings/schools in Wales have a duty towards present and prospective children to provide an inclusive curriculum that will offer opportunities for all children to achieve their full potential in preparation for further learning and life. For children with disabilities in particular, they should make reasonable adjustments.
> (Department for Children, Education, Lifelong Learning and Skills, 2008, p. 2)

It seems clear that any future legislation or policy relating to the early years and children with SEN will continue to acknowledge the role early years settings have in developing inclusion, particularly as 'High-quality pre-school programmes lead to stronger and more enduring effects on outcomes, especially for disadvantaged children, boys and children with special educational needs' (DfE/DoH, 2011, p. 62).

Partnership with parents

The general theme of partnership with parents has underpinned many recent developments in the early years sector, and consulting with families has been regarded as key to effective engagement. More specifically, parental involvement, responsibility and inclusion in both decision making and service delivery has been an integral part of all the legislation and guidance on SEN. There has been recognition in policies that the impact of any support 'is undermined if it doesn't reflect each family's unique circumstances. Parents know their child best' (DfE, 2011a, p. 41).

Within the Codes of Practice in all four principalities of the United Kingdom, partnership with parents has been defined in the following terms.

Sharing information. Parents should be made fully aware of support services and the processes around providing support that a setting will follow. All information around the provision for children with special needs should be accessible and understandable. Within a local authority there should be a key person or Parent Partnership Service that parents contact regarding issues around SEN. Within a setting a Special Needs Co-ordinator takes on the responsibility of being a central contact and the provision is also required to make available a SEN policy document. There should be clarity around how the staged process of assessment works and how this may be initiated.

Involvement in assessment. The views of parents should be actively sought when working towards solutions for their children. This relates to every stage of the process of responding to the child's requirements, from the plans for beginning at the setting to the work around transition to school. Table 2.2 shows in detail an example of the key principles of involving parents, taken from the Code of Practice relating to the 2009 Additional Support for Learning Act in Scotland.

Decision making. Parents must be involved in all decision making, from the initial stages of providing additional support in the setting to bringing in other agencies for advice. Parents will be central to any decision to move on to more formal assessment required for a Statement of Special Educational Needs/Education, Health and Care

Table 2.2 From the Code of Practice/Additional Support for Learning Act 2009

Professionals should:
- acknowledge and draw on parental knowledge and expertise in relation to their child
- consider the child's strengths as well as areas of additional need
- recognise the personal and emotional investment of parents and be aware of their feelings
- ensure that parents understand procedures, are aware of how to access support and are given documents to be discussed well in advance of meetings
- respect the validity of differing perspectives and seek constructive ways of reconciling different viewpoints
- cater for the differing needs parents may have, such as those arising from a disability, or communication and linguistic barriers.

Information should be:
- clear and understandable and avoid jargon
- provided easily in accessible formats
- readily available and provided automatically without a charge and without a fuss.

Communication works well when:
- people have the interpreters they need
- someone in authority takes responsibility for keeping parents up-to-date
- people are told what has been happening between meetings
- any information provided by parents is acknowledged
- formal references to statutory procedures are avoided.

Effective working relationships develop when:
- contact with parents is sensitive, positive, helpful and regular
- parents feel included and are encouraged to contribute to discussions
- positive, clear and easily understood language is used
- parents are involved and processes and roles are explained from the beginning
- parents are told what to expect and the next steps
- times of meeting take account of parents' availability.

Meetings work best when:
- parents are asked what times and places suit them best, taking account of any access need or family responsibilities
- notes from meetings, and any papers to be considered, are sent out in good time
- parents are invited to add points to the agenda, at the same time as everyone else
- people attending are aware of their roles and the roles of others and they understand the child's or young person's additional support needs
- there are no hidden issues, and no last minute surprises
- decisions are made when parents are at the meeting, or agreed with them before the meeting takes place, not after the meeting has closed, unless further consultation takes place with them
- ample time is given to allow people time to raise concerns, so that decisions are not rushed.

Identifying the way forward works well when:
- all views are taken on board – including those of the child or young person
- people are interested in learning from each other
- people show an interest in general family priorities and take them on board
- services are identified in agreement with the family and are responsive to individual needs.

Accountability and involvement:
- who is responsible for what is clearly defined and understood
- parents concerns are responded to quickly
- decisions are open to scrutiny
- parents have a clear point of contact who can answer questions, make decisions and ensure that agreed actions are taken
- people do what they agreed within the timescale committed to – if a decision is likely to take time, parents are told and given some idea of when

Source: Scottish Government, 2009.

Plan (in England, Wales and Northern Ireland) or Co-ordinated Support Plan (in Scotland). This is most likely to happen during a child's pre-school years at the time of moving into school. Parents have rights to choose schools within the formal process and to appeal against the level of provision made by the local authority at this stage. Access to independent tribunals is available for parents if mutually acceptable arrangements cannot be made through mediation and negotiation with the authorities.

The overall focus on parents as partners in shaping their services seems likely to sharpen as policies and legislation develops. In 2011 the English government's Green Paper 'Support and Aspiration: a new approach to special educational needs and disability', highlighted the benefits of the Early Support Programme with its emphasis on Family Service plans and parent-held records. The vision for parent partnership seemed to be shifting parents much more to the centre of decision making, with the aim of families eventually being given the option of control over purchasing their own support services for their child through a personalised budget system. By having control over which health, social care and even education support services they choose, parents could potentially be much more influential in shaping their child's daily lives and future opportunities.

Involvement of children

There has been recognition in legislation and guidance in the early years sector that:

> All children and young people should have the opportunity to make their views known about decisions which affect them [and that] they need to know that what they have to say will be respected, listened to and, where appropriate, acted on.
>
> (Scottish Government, 2009)

In the 2006 Childcare Act, local authorities in England were placed under a new duty to take into account the views of young children when making arrangements within early childhood services. This was in line with Article 12 of the UN Convention on the Rights of the Child, in particular General Comment 7 'Implementing Child Rights in Early Childhood', which stressed the importance of respecting the views of younger as well as older children. Taking account of what young people say they need has been a principle reflected in all the Codes of Practice for children with SEN. There has also been an acknowledgement that consultation with young children requires a range of strategies in addition to verbal communication in order to include in the process young children with special needs and those children who are pre-verbal (DENI, 2005).

The 2009 guidance for the Additional Support for Learning Act in Scotland highlighted the importance of schools and early years settings creating a climate where children's participation in decision making was an everyday activity. In such an environment the outlook that all children had views and could communicate them in some way would develop. For very young children such decision making is nurtured through being given the opportunity to make choices and learning to adjust these in response to other peers and adults. Significantly, these skills have been identified as key aspects of early learning (DfES, 2007) and continue to be highlighted whenever a National Curriculum is reframed (Tickell, 2011).

Multi-disciplinary working

The need to communicate, collaborate and co-ordinate has been an increasingly strong theme throughout the legislation, particularly with policy initiatives such as *Every Child Matters* or *Getting it Right for Every Child* and legislation such as the 2004 Children's Act. There has been a recognition that collaboration between organisations and agencies needs to be at the structural level, as well as in response to individual needs, and that links must be formally strengthened between health, education and social services as well as independent and voluntary agencies. In Scotland, for example, the Early Years Framework launched in 2008 focused on encouraging joint working between the public, private and voluntary sectors because it was recognised that much innovative and flexible support work can take place outside the constraints of the public service sector.

In England, Wales and Northern Ireland, Children's Centres, whether stand-alone or based within schools or other established settings, have remained central to developing co-located services with shared principles and practices. This important role was highlighted in the 'Supporting Families in the Foundation Years' report in England (DfE/DoH, 2011), the 'Early Years (0–6) Strategy' in Northern Ireland (DENI, 2010) and in the Welsh Assembly's 'Flying Start' programme. Beyond the Children's Centres, early years practitioners in pre-schools and nurseries in England were positioned at the centre of a collaborative working initiative with health visitors as part of the 'Healthy Child Programme' (DfE/DoH, 2011). Within this programme early years settings were to contribute to every child's developmental review at 2.5 years old, either directly or by sharing, with parents' permission, the EYFS progress check carried out for each child.

For children with SEN and their families, in particular, there has been a history of fragmentation and competition between departments, which at times has led to parents having to co-ordinate services themselves. In recognition of this issue a commitment was made in England to build on the Early Support approach of developing a 'team around the child' with a designated keyworker to co-ordinate services for individual families. Significantly, the 'Support and Aspiration' policy document that announced this plan proposed that keyworkers would be trained 'from a wider field of professionals with relevant knowledge about working with families and about disabled children and children with SEN' (DfE, 2011a, p. 43). This underlines that multi-disciplinary working is likely to remain an important dimension of any strategies put in place to support young children and their families.

Workforce development

A final theme evident in legislation and policy development within the early years sector has been the development of a better trained and qualified workforce. In both England and Scotland in recent years there has been a drive to invest in graduate-level training in early education and childcare, with an aspiration of having leaders of early years centres or provision hold a degree qualification (DfE/DoH, 2011;

Scottish Government/COSLA, 2008). The significance of training lead practitioners with expertise in both early intervention and special needs has also been highlighted as part of the national qualification for the leaders of Children's Centres (DfE, 2011a). By 2011 a review of early education and childcare qualifications in England reported that the majority of staff in group-based childcare settings outside schools (76 per cent) had a relevant qualification at least to level 3, and 8 per cent had a relevant level 6 qualification. The Early Years Professional status that was introduced in 2005 was also found to be having an impact on both the skill level and status of practitioners (DfE, 2011b).

A further review of qualifications and training within the early years workforce lead by Professor Cathy Nutbrown (DfE, 2012c) highlighted the need for training to 'equip people with the skills they need to successfully support disabled children and children with SEN' (DfE, 2012b, p. 17). As the new qualifications of 'Early Years Teacher' and 'Early Years Educator' emerged in 2013 as a response to the Nutbrown review (DfE, 2013), it seems likely that the new training framework would retain a focus on SEN.

Multi-disciplinary working has long been regarded as a significant factor in developing a workforce with the skills to support a wide range of children. Policy documents often highlight how different practitioners can learn new approaches by working alongside one another (DfE/DoH, 2011). The value of introducing more general training programmes for the whole workforce has also featured in initiatives pushing forward professional development. In autumn 2007 in England the Department for Education launched the Inclusion Development Programme (IDP), which was designed to strengthen the confidence and expertise of early years practitioners in supporting children with SEN. Over a three-year period materials were made widely available, looking at supporting: children with speech, language and communication needs; autism; and behavioural, emotional and social difficulties. Similarly, the 'Every Child a Talker' materials and training initiative launched in 2008 encouraged at local authority and practitioner level the development of support for early communication development. By 2012 the government in England were looking to use this model to further embed effective practice as part of workforce development, training early years practitioners in Children's Centres to support children under three identified as 'at risk' from language delay.

Summary

The legislative and policy context that continues to evolve shows that the needs of young children have gained an increasingly high profile for governments and administrators. Consequently, there is continued pressure on services to raise quality, work more effectively and co-ordinate their efforts. At different times services will be well resourced to meet such demands, but at other times the general economic climate may make the effective delivery much more difficult. Whatever the situation that practitioners find themselves in, it is likely that the themes that have been outlined in this chapter will shape the nature of the support they provide. Good practice will be built upon: promoting children's rights; providing support as early as possible; assessing requirements effectively; developing inclusion in the local community; working together with parents and other services; taking account of children's views; and engaging with professional development.

Case study: The CAN approach to assessment – early years SEND team in Blackpool

The English government's Green Paper 'Support and Aspiration: a new approach to special educational needs and disability' (DfE, 2011a) identified a number of shortcomings with the statutory assessment process. These included the length of time that the process took (often over six months from the time of initial discussions to final decisions) and its adversarial nature, pushing parents and local authorities into a struggle over appropriate resources and provision. In different areas of the country professionals at strategic and practitioner level have developed innovative ways of working with the statutory procedure in order to attempt to address some of these issues. The early years SEND team in Blackpool wanted the process to 'account for dynamic early development' (Shannon and Cooper, 2013) rather than be a collection of 'snapshot' assessments of the child by the various professionals involved. The team felt that for young children currency and coherence were vital and that families should be at the centre of all the planning, rather than on the periphery of the process. Consequently, the team began to develop the 'Chronicle of Additional Need' (CAN) to underpin the statutory assessment of young children with SEN in their authority.

The CAN approach begins with a collective meeting of parents and all the practitioners involved. Drawing on the multiple perspectives presented, the aim is to record or 'chronicle' the child's current skills, knowledge and understanding. The focus is on day-to-day issues such as feeding, sleep routines or medication, as well as developmental progress within the EYFS. In addition to developing a collective view on the current situation, the process also focuses on agreeing future positive learning outcomes for the child. Significantly, the CAN also records the additional resources, provision or support that may be required for the child to achieve these outcomes and which agency or professional will be responsible for delivering this service. A review cycle is negotiated during this initial period based on the child and family's individual situation and the timeframe around future transition to nursery or school.

The central idea behind the CAN approach is that it will be an established joint planning and assessment cycle for young children identified with SEN. The intention is for it to feed into the statutory assessment process, providing much more holistic and formative basis for any formal procedure. Most importantly, the parents will have had the opportunity to be at the centre of the CAN process and the long-term planning for their child. They will have been involved with the professionals that support them over an extended period of time, negotiating and understanding what their child needs to progress. Consequently they are less likely to be suddenly confronted with people's opinions or difficult decisions about the choices available to them.

During the pilot stage of using the CAN approach in Blackpool over 20 children were assessed in this way. The CANs were used to help plan for transition into schools and also to access specialist settings without the need for additional time-consuming assessments. The records also proved useful for Social Services to inform the fostering and adoption procedure for some children. The feedback from families involved was very positive. They generally felt very much more aware about what was happening and how decisions were made. Crucially, parents also reported that they had a voice in the process and that their opinion was valued.

Chapter 3

Roles and responsibilities

A network of support

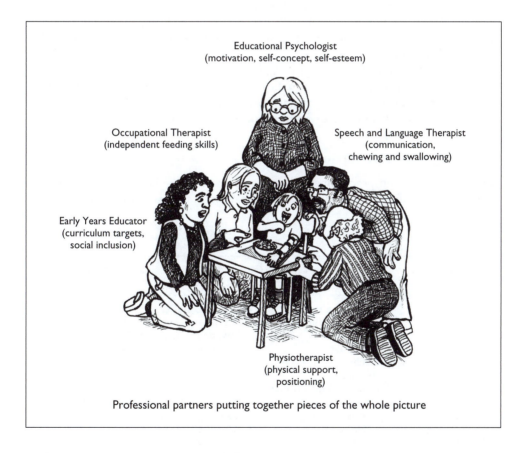

Educational Psychologist
(motivation, self-concept, self-esteem)

Occupational Therapist
(independent feeding skills)

Speech and Language Therapist
(communication,
chewing and swallowing)

Early Years Educator
(curriculum targets,
social inclusion)

Physiotherapist
(physical support,
positioning)

Professional partners putting together pieces of the whole picture

One of the features of good collaboration is clarity about what different professionals do, how they do it and with whom. Everyone then knows where to go for specific advice and this helps reduce duplication and ensure appropriate referrals are made. Clarity about roles and responsibilities also gives realistic expectations about what is on offer. One misconception is the extent to which professionals will be involved in 'hands-on' casework. Often the role of professionals is to assess a child's needs and suggest appropriate strategies, but they will not necessarily be the people providing the delivery. Not only do services not have the resources to do this, but interventions are less intrusive when they happen in a routine way with familiar adults. Although specific support may be required, it is equally important that any overall approach is developed within the context of the child's everyday experiences and interactions. Consequently, professionals usually prioritise consulting with parents and early years practitioners about ways of meeting the child's needs at home and school, as well as offering a direct service when this is indicated.

A major issue for children with special needs, their families and those working to support them can be the sheer number of professionals involved. Table 3.1 shows the range of services identified by parents in relation to caring for their disabled children (Campbell-Hall *et al.*, 2009):

Negotiating and understanding these networks can be a daunting task. Of course, not all children and families will be utilising this number of services at any one time. Some need an intensive level of additional support from multiple agencies, while others will be supported by maybe one or two additional professionals (Early Support, 2012). Similarly, the level of support may vary for each child at any one time depending on circumstances, situations and emerging needs. For example, when a young person identified with special needs moves from pre-school into primary school more people may be involved to support this transition.

Getting good information

For both families and practitioners alike, understanding the boundaries of roles and responsibilities starts with having basic information on the range of services on offer.

Table 3.1

Health care services	Education services	Care and family support services	Multi-agency services
• GP • Pharmacist • Optician • Health visitor • Community nurse • Speech therapist • Occupational therapist • Paediatrician • Dermatologist • Psychiatrist • Dietician • Physiotherapist • Surgeon • Consultant	• School nurse • Head teacher • Classroom support • School behavioural classes • Special educational needs co-ordinator (SENCO) • Connexions • Outreach team • Educational psychologist • Visual impairment teaching team	• Financial benefits (Disability Living Allowance; Carer's Allowance; grants) • Social worker • Counselling services • Local support groups • National charities – e.g. ASBAH (Association for Spina Bifida and Hydrocephalus)	• Parent Partnership Officers • Child Development Centres • Children and Adolescent Mental Health Services (CAMHS)

Source: adapted from Campbell-Hall *et al.*, 2009, p. 7.

Many services provide web-based information that gives an overview of expectations. In best practice, such resources are translated into community languages. Sure Start Children's Centres are also required to offer a localised hub where families can readily access information about support services (DfE, 2012d). Most services provide open information about what they provide, how they work and how they can be contacted. Others offer more limited information that can sometimes lead to assumptions and/or raise false hopes. Transparency about services that defines terminology and is unambiguous is therefore best practice.

Besides the quality of information, there is the issue of who controls dissemination. Although open access to the internet is helpful, professionals sometimes put themselves in the position of 'gate-keepers' choosing when to guide families towards different services or support. Such judgements may be made to prevent information overload for a family seen to be under stress. From a parental perspective, however, such practices could be counter-productive and disempowering:

> I know there are mothers/families out there who wouldn't have appreciated involvement from others but surely parents of disabled children should have the information immediately and decide themselves if and when they contact someone for help??? I was made to feel useless and completely unable to cope with all that comes with having a disabled child – if I had been given maybe just a leaflet when leaving hospital I could have a point of reference when I felt things weren't going great. I could have been in control of who I contacted and when I contacted them.
>
> (A parent carer in Ashford, cited in Early Support, 2012, p. 30)

With the development of family-centred plans as part of the multi-disciplinary approach for children with complex needs, parents are less likely to be marginalised and will have an increasingly central role as decision makers and sometimes budget holders. When linking with parents for the first time, however, practitioners should not expect the family to be the source of all information about the agencies they use for their child. It is a key responsibility for early years settings to develop knowledge of services for themselves and apply such awareness to the individual situations they encounter.

The real world

Although this chapter gives a general overview of roles and responsibilities, not all services operate in the same way. There continue to be wide regional variations, both in the resources available and in the specific activities undertaken. We are also living in a time of considerable change and development, with new legislation and guidance in special education, early years provision, social services and community health. It would be wise to check with local services for details of how they work in your area. Appendix 1 provides a starting point for finding out about services and organisations for young disabled children or those with special needs and their families.

Although in this chapter we describe individual roles, good inter-agency work is often built on positive working relationships that enable practitioners to move beyond rigid role definitions. Best practice develops where professionals focus on the needs of the child and family, share what has to be done and decide jointly who is doing what. People who are hidebound by their job description may lack the flexibility that working with complex situations might need. Planning must be based on the most sensible thing to do for this child in this situation, with the resources and skills available. When people share responsibilities, challenges and solutions, they gain a better understanding not only of the pressures others are working under but also the possibilities that exist.

Health professionals

Since 2009 in England and Northern Ireland, the government's Healthy Child Programme framed the early intervention and prevention strategy for children from birth to 19 years of age. Scotland revised their Child Health Systems Programme in 2011, and by 2012 the Welsh Assembly were exploring parallel strategies within their 'Reproductive and Early Years Pathfinders'. A common feature of these core frameworks is to establish a model of service delivery that differentiates between those available to everyone (universal) and additional services that will be provided according to need. It is useful to think about the range of health professionals that can be involved with young children identified with special needs and their families in this way.

Universal services

Health visitors take a primary role in supporting and monitoring the development of all young children. They are qualified nurses or midwives who have additional training and expertise in child health. Health visitors are 'skilled at spotting early issues, which may develop into problems or risks to the family if not addressed' (Department of Health, 2011, p. 7). They take the lead in co-ordinating a series of developmental checks or reviews critical in identifying children and families requiring early support. A schedule of universal checks from England is shown in Table 3.2.

Families hold their own Personal Child Health Record (or the 'red book'), where details of the reviews are kept. These can be shared with other professionals at the

Table 3.2 Universal checks

New baby review at 14 days	A face-to-face review with parents and child.
Review at 6–8 weeks	Includes a full physical check and discussion about development.
Review at one year	Assessment of child's physical, social and emotional needs in the context of the family.
Review at 2–2½ years	Involves child and parents – covering social, emotional, behavioural and language development. The two-year progress review carried out by early years settings should link with this check.
Review at 4–5 years	Health assessment on entry to school either in reception or Year 1 in conjunction with the school nurse service. Includes hearing and vision screening.

family's discretion and added to if their child has additional appointments or involvement with other services.

As well as providing support and advice for families themselves, health visitors also act as the gateway to other support services. It is often the health visitor who makes the initial referral to services such as Portage or speech therapy. Health visitors are increasingly seen as part of an early years team and, although historically based in general practitioner surgeries, are now often co-located with other relevant professionals in Sure Start Children's Centres. The Health Visiting Implementation Plan (Department of Health, 2011) in England envisaged the health visitor becoming 'leaders of child health locally', linking families with both community services and other parents.

School nursing services take over from health visitors as the universal health-monitoring agency for children once they are of school age. All schools have an allocated school nurse, although the visiting schedule may differ considerably from one institution to another. Often, the health visitor will liaise with pre-school provision about individuals, but the school nurse may also be able to offer ongoing support, especially if the child is in a nursery attached to a school or in the reception year. Both health visitors and school nurses are valuable to include in a meeting for a child with SEN who is starting school and has medical needs which require monitoring and intervention. The school nursing service often covers a large number of schools and consists of nurses working as a team. The team members are likely to have different areas of expertise in supporting children with various needs or in child health promotion.

Other universal services include the *general practitioner* (GP), who is a 'family doctor' working in the community. Often, families will be registered with a group practice or health centre rather than a named doctor. For many families, the GP may be the first point of contact if they have concerns about their child's wellbeing. GPs can also validate a family's welfare or disability benefit application if appropriate. While primarily focusing on the child's health, the GP can also refer on to other more specialised support services.

Additional or specialist health services

There are generally two pathways to more specialised services (Early Support, 2010a). If a child's birth has been complicated and required a longer than usual stay in hospital or if a condition associated with impairments is diagnosed, such as Down syndrome, a hospital discharge meeting will usually take place. This involves all the professionals who have cared for the child in hospital, practitioners from the community nursing team and parents. The aim is to plan the support the family requires for their child on returning home.

In addition to the universal services described earlier, a specialist health visitor with experience in supporting families with young disabled children at home may be introduced to them. The paediatrician who has overseen the child's medical care in the neo-natal unit will probably refer on to specialists in other hospitals for ongoing expert advice. For some families this can result in a continuous commitment to attend numerous appointments at different hospital clinics or tertiary centres during the child's early years. In many areas the family will be referred on to a more local *child development centre* (CDC) or *child development team* (CDT). Referral to this centre provides access to assessment and support from a multi-disciplinary team of health professionals and other services.

The second pathway to involvement with the CDT is through the universal developmental check schedule described earlier. This process endeavours to pick up on issues during the early years and prompt health professionals in consultation with the family to refer on to other specialists. Seeking further advice and support does not have to be delayed until these designated review times; parents are encouraged to discuss concerns at any time with their GP, health visitor or support staff at their local Children's Centre. Practitioners in early years settings also have a responsibility to respond to parents' concerns by guiding them to other agencies as appropriate. They also play a role in monitoring children's development within their groups and sensitively raising issues with families.

The child development team

Whichever the pathway to specialist services, a *community paediatrician* is likely to be involved, as well as the hospital-based specialists. The community paediatrician is usually in charge of the CDC or CDT and co-ordinates a group of medical professionals such as other doctors, speech therapists, occupational therapists, physiotherapists, clinical psychologists and specialist health visitors. They will also refer on to appropriate specialists as required.

Other professionals in the CDT are responsible for carrying out regular developmental reviews for individual children and also contribute to medical advice in any formal assessments that take place before a child starts school. A family's involvement with any of these professionals may include regular therapy sessions for their child, either in a clinic or at home. CDTs commonly consist of the following:

*   *Speech and language therapists* (SLTs) assess, diagnose and develop programmes to help children develop communication skills (Early Support, 2010b, p. 10). Their focus is on communication in the broadest sense, including the use of spoken language, signs, symbols or communication aids. Some SLTs may also have specific expertise in supporting children with eating or swallowing difficulties. They work directly with parents and children, but also in an advisory role for other professionals and early years settings. An SLT often receives referrals from different routes as well as being part of the CDT.
*   *Physiotherapists* have expertise in supporting children's physical and motor development. They can be involved with children from birth, particularly if the baby has experienced early complications that are likely to lead to physical impairments. They can also provide advice for parents and practitioners with regards to handling and positioning during everyday activities such as feeding or dressing. Early years settings may encounter a physiotherapist working in this advisory capacity when supporting the inclusion of individual children in their groups.
*   *Occupational therapists* (OTs) aim to support optimum activity for individuals in their everyday lives. For children they can be concerned with wide-ranging

Table 3.3 Other professionals

Dietician	Provides advice about nutrition, particularly for babies and young children with feeding difficulties. They may be especially involved in supporting parents to care for their children who require feeding via nasogastric tube or gastronomy at home.
Audiologist	Carries out hearing tests and relays the results to parents. They advise on the wearing of hearing aids and monitor hearing for children. They can refer on to other specialists as required.
Opthalmologist	Specialises in the diagnosis and treatment of eye defects and diseases. As doctors they will see young children to treat eye disorders with appropriate medicine or surgery.
Orthoptist	Tests children's eyesight and work on developing functional eye movements for children who have squints. This is primarily through prescribing glasses and advising on visual exercises.

activities such as assessing the most functional seating for them to sit at a table or working out which adapted cup will allow them to drink without assistance. OTs can be employed either by the Health Service or by Social Services, but those attached to the CDT are likely to be part of the former and have specialist paediatric expertise. These OTs provide advice on how a child's motor or perceptual difficulties will affect their learning and offer strategies to support their inclusion in pre-school activities. OTs employed by Social Services can become increasingly involved as a child grows older as they focus on what is required for the young person to take part in everyday routines.

Other professionals who might be involved with families through their connection with the CDT are shown in Table 3.3.

Significantly, in England the 'core purpose' of local Sure Start Children's Centres has developed to include linking with other specialist services (DfE, 2012d). Consequently, a child and family may see their speech therapist or physiotherapist in this location rather than visiting a specialised centre.

Additional education services

In the same way as there are universal and additional services for young children identified with special needs within the health sector, within early years education a further layer of support is available beyond general access to pre-schools, nurseries and child-minders.

Portage

Portage (named after the town in the United States from which it originated) is a home-visiting educational service for young children identified with SEN and their families. The service offers regular home visits, weekly or fortnightly, by a trained Portage home visitor. The aim of each visit is to decide on a learning activity that the family practise and enjoy together. The activities are based on play and the everyday routines of individual families. When Portage visits begin, profiles or developmental checklists can be used to identify strengths and goals for future learning. Other professionals often make joint visits with Portage visitors and may contribute to action plans for the child. Portage services often work closely with the early years setting that a child attends.

All Portage workers have basic Portage training accredited by the National Portage Association and many will have received advanced training. This training is often open to other early years practitioners, although priority is given to those taking up positions as home visitors. Portage has been established in the UK since 1975, and by 2012 there were around 140 services spread throughout the country. The majority of Portage services are local authority funded and managed within the structure of children or education services. The services can be based in Sure Start centres or may run group play sessions for children using the service in these facilities. Some have also been set up within the voluntary sector.

Educational psychologists

Most educational psychologists (EPs) are employed by a local authority and will be part of an educational psychology service (EPS) within that region. The EPS is itself usually part of Children's Services or education departments within their local authority. Educational psychologists work with early years settings and schools, providing advice to enhance learning, social and emotional development for children who require additional support. They work in partnership with parents, teachers and other professionals, and although they may get to know individual families well over time, they rarely work directly with individual children on a long-term basis. EPs may also work more generally in a consultative role. This could cover devising strategies for managing behaviour with a staff group or providing training on working with parents or involving children in decision making.

The EP can be a useful resource for both parents and those working in the early years. He or she will have extensive knowledge about aspects of child development, learning and SEN. They are familiar with assessment procedures and can provide information about the processes involved in gaining access to the range of provision available. They may also be able to judge the extent to which the child meets any criteria for accessing different levels of support and suggest realistic expectations in terms of educational requirements. The EP has a central role in providing written advice within the formal assessment process leading to an Education and Health Care Plan (in England) or an IEP in Scotland (see Chapter 2). Their preliminary assessments are key factors when local authorities decide whether the formal process needs to be initiated to further support the child's ongoing SEN.

Specialist teachers

Young children may also be supported by specialist teachers who visit the child at home and often in their pre-school setting. These teachers will usually be part of a local authority early years sensory support or SEN team and they work in close partnership with families and practitioners. Because they are not based in one place they are often referred to as visiting or peripatetic teachers. Their role is usually advisory and they either have particular experience in working with children with learning difficulties in the early years or training in teaching children with specific impairments. Specific specialist teaching roles that children, families and practitioners may encounter in the early years are set out in Table 3.4.

Referrals to specialist teachers are usually via CDTs or directly from hospital specialists who were involved in diagnosing specific impairments. When a child starts at an early years setting, staff need to liaise with any specialist teachers and invite these professionals to a pre-entry meeting. Settings can be proactive in making these links with the support of parents who have the necessary contact details.

The advice that specialist teachers can provide at transition enables any adjustments and arrangements to be made in order to support the child's inclusion. For example, the teacher of a child with visual impairment will be able to explain what this means for their learning, as well as how to adapt the environment. This could include using specific materials, print size, positioning, mobility, access to activities, room layout and so on. Similarly, a teacher of the hearing impaired will be able to discuss the implications that the child's deafness may have for her play, education and social interactions generally. It will be important to discuss functional hearing. The sense that the child may make of language in a lively classroom may be different from that in a room with optimal acoustics. For young children in particular, the practice suggested for children with hearing difficulties is good educational practice for all children – such as ensuring children are looking at you before speaking to them and giving visual support for new vocabulary.

Table 3.4 Specialist teaching roles

Teacher of children with multi-sensory impairments	A teacher of children with multi-sensory impairments has received specialist training and usually holds a relevant qualification. They support children, their family and other teachers in homes and settings.
Teacher of children with visual impairments (QTVI)	A teacher of children with visual impairments has received specialist training and holds a qualification to work with children with visual impairments. In the pre-school years, they visit and support families and children in their homes.
Teacher of the deaf (ToD)/teacher of the hearing impaired	A teacher of the deaf has received specialist training and holds a qualification to work with hearing-impaired children. They support children, their families and other professionals involved with a child's education. Peripatetic teachers of the deaf travel to the family home and to playgroups, nurseries, schools and colleges. Some teachers of the deaf have additional training to work with very young children.

Source: adapted from Early Support, 2010b, p. 10.

The specialist teaching services may also provide a monitoring role for children throughout their school life, starting with the early years. They may visit a setting to observe and discuss the child's progress with parents and practitioners. How often they visit may depend on the child's specific needs and the level of support he is receiving from other agencies. There is also likely to be joint visiting, especially with other key professionals who work regularly with the family at home, such as Portage workers.

Other additional professionals

All local authorities throughout the UK are required to fund a *Parent Partnership Service* for families to offer impartial information, advice and support for parents/ carers of children and young people identified with SEN. The Parent Partnership Service will also provide an *independent parent supporter* if families wish, who is trained specifically to support parents in understanding the SEN Code of Practice. Independent parent supporters are usually volunteers with some background experience of the SEN system. They can play a particularly significant role if a young child is being formally assessed by the local authority. Independent supporters can accompany parents to meetings as well as facilitate their participation in the whole process. Since 2010 in England there have been moves to shift Parent Partnership Services away from their connections with local authorities towards more integration with the voluntary sector. This was seen to be a significant move in order to ensure that parents were receiving more transparent and independent advice on provision and their options.

Voluntary organisations

Voluntary agencies can be either local or national, and either umbrella organisations, such as those campaigning for inclusive education, or aligned with specific needs. They have a significant and increasing role in the education and support of children with SEN and their families at several different levels. Voluntary agencies may provide, co-ordinate or contribute the following:

- information, e.g. websites, publications, conferences, training programmes.
- family support, which is usually provided by local groups, e.g. AFASIC (Association for All Speech Impaired Children), NAS (National Autistic Society) and DSA (Down Syndrome Association) all have a network of local branches which support parents regionally.
- short break support, e.g. Scope provide a range of options in different locations that includes after-school schemes, access to leisure facilities, home-based and community support.
- individual advice and support on specific issues; this is often provided through helplines such as those run by Scope or the NAS. Both of these charities have established parent-support schemes that link families of disabled children together. 'Face2Face' (Scope, 2012) or Parent to Parent Service/P2P (NAS, 2013) are examples of this provision.
- outreach workers supporting families, e.g. 'Sense', the national charity for deaf-blind people and their families, have specialist advisory teachers and therapists who can visit families and settings to provide specific advice, information and training.

- local authority policy making; representatives of the voluntary sector are increasingly consulted with or participate directly in policy development. Third-party organisations are often involved at a strategic level with local authorities through their capacity as members of a Children's Trust Board, which brings together children's services in a locality to plan provision and joint support.
- pressure groups; these use the media, conferences and other events to raise the profile of the changes that they would like to see.
- research and training; major national organisations are often involved in carrying out research activities within the remit of their concerns. Sometimes they decide on areas of investigation and bid for funding; at other times government departments or universities may ask for their contributions.

Appendix 1 includes contact details for many of these voluntary organisations.

All professionals need to be aware of local group support and make sure parents are informed. Where voluntary agencies are involved in direct work with children, it is helpful for professionals to liaise so there is collaborative and complementary support.

Social services

Social service departments are usually organised in teams, and in a local authority will be part of Children's Services. As a statutory service their universal role is to 'support children in need, protect them from significant harm and promote the safety and wellbeing of children who live at home or who are in the public care system' (Early Support, 2010c, p. 2). Since the Children Act in 1989 local authorities have been required to provide for children 'in need' in their locality, a definition that includes children who are disabled and those whose development is causing concern. Many local authorities have a 'children with disabilities' team that concentrates on supporting families with disabled children. Some families may be put in touch with a social worker when they leave hospital with their baby, particularly if they have spent time in the special care baby unit. A hospital social worker may have made a referral to the community social work team. Many families, however, will mainly have support via health- and education-based services in their child's first years.

Social service support is much more extensive than their highly publicised role in safeguarding children. They provide a wide range of services either directly or by commissioning other providers. Services for children with special needs can include:

- arranging, funding or providing short breaks for children, either with their families or in specialist residential centres. Since 2010 in England local authorities are required to publish details of their short break provision and plans for developing these services.
- help at home with the daily routines and physical care of the child. *Family support workers* may work in the home or in a Children's Centre, providing a range of practical help and advice. Their support is likely to focus on the whole family, including the siblings of the child identified with special needs. Such support workers may be linked with a family from a local Children's Centre base, rather than provided for families by Social Services.

- funding for assessments and adaptions to the home (for example, for bathrooms or sleeping facilities).
- access to specialist child-minders.
- access to a 'home child carer' service where a trained person comes to look after the child for short periods at home.
- advice on benefits and eligibility for the Disabled Facilities Grant, which can contribute to the costs of any adaption that needs to be made to the family home.

The level of support available from social services is usually subject to an initial assessment against set eligibility criteria. If a family is eligible for support for their child, then a further 'core' assessment will take place to decide which services need to be provided in the family's circumstances. Parents can also choose to put their children's names on the local authority's Children with Disabilities Register. This gives families access to regular information about such things as holiday play-schemes, local support groups and short break arrangements. The register also helps services in the local authority to plan for future needs and monitor the availability of provision.

Case study: Paul's story – building a support team

At 28 weeks, Paul was born extremely prematurely and spent his first five weeks in intensive care receiving specialist medical support from the neonatology team. As a result of birth trauma the vision part of his brain was damaged by a cerebral haemorrhage. Consequently, appropriate professionals, including an ophthalmologist, became involved and as his condition stabilised he was transferred to a second hospital for a further eight-week stay. A breast-feeding specialist also supported the family at this time. As his discharge from hospital approached, Paul's family was introduced to the community nurse responsible for supporting them at home. Paul was still oxygen-dependent, which meant that an early focus for everyone was the administration of oxygen at home as well as ensuring that his parents could cope with the routine medical procedures themselves. Paul's mum Julie describes one aspect of the community nurse's role as gradually 'weaning us from hospital care' with the frequency of her visits slowly decreasing over a three-month period. The transition also involved routing medical support for Paul through the family's GP and the paediatric outreach services at his local hospital. Referrals to physiotherapy, speech and language therapy and occupational therapy all happened at this time, requiring new, regular commitments to consultation sessions with these therapists. A dietician also provided key input and advice during this period because of the ongoing issues with feeding and weaning Paul.

As the professional team supporting Paul and his family expanded, investigations continued into the extent and nature of his visual impairment. Following a local ophthalmology consultation he was referred to a London hospital for more specialised assessment, and at 11 months old, as a result of this assessment and the diagnosis of cerebral visual impairment, Paul was registered 'severely sight impaired (blind)'. Following this more formal diagnosis the sensory support team that was part of the local authority's Children's Services began to provide regular ongoing support to the family. When Paul was six months old his community nurse also made a referral to the local Portage service and the family started receiving regular home visits three months later. Julie recalls that it was the Portage visitor that helped the family draw together the increasingly complex network of services and professionals involved through initiating a 'team around the child' (TAC) meeting. Since regular Portage support discontinued on Paul's starting nursery, Julie has taken responsibility for convening the TAC meetings herself, chairing the group and recording the agreed actions in written minutes. Currently a range of professionals are committed to attending the meetings, including Paul's physiotherapist, OT, sensory support team teacher, SLT, nursery supervisor and early years advisory teacher.

Julie feels her 'enquiring' nature has also motivated her to seek out complementary support in addition to that provided by the statutory agencies. For example, she engaged a physiotherapist with particular expertise in working with children with complex needs and visual impairment for Paul. Recently she has also arranged music therapy sessions for him. From Julie's perspective, professionals working with children with low incidence disabilities may themselves face a 'learning curve' and consequently broadening the range of expertise within the support team is helpful for everyone. Similarly, voluntary organisations have played an important role in offering supplementary support to the family. The National Society for Blind Children (NSBC), Royal National Institute for the Blind (RNIB) and a local trust organisation for families of children with visual impairment have all been involved, providing wide-ranging advice from completing benefit applications to educational provision. These charities have also facilitated contact with other parents at group meetings for Paul's family. Julie sees such organisations as having ongoing significance for Paul as he gets older.

Paul has been at nursery since he was two and a half years old and his speech and communication skills have developed greatly in the six months that he has been attending. During Paul's first month at the nursery, a mobility officer carried out an environmental audit to highlight any changes that would need to be made to ensure Paul's safe access and participation in the sessions despite his low vision and need for support when walking. Julie says he enjoys 'usual little boy things' such as playing with cars and 'Thomas the Tank Engine'. He likes painting and water play as well as walking around climbing frames and venturing up the ladder with some help. As his vision is still developing he examines objects close up with great care and concentration. He is still getting used to the rush and tumble of children around him, but Julie says he is usually very confident around adults. She does not find this surprising as he has become accustomed to having 'a lot of adults in his life at close proximity'.

Keyworkers

The range and complexity of the network of practitioners and services is highlighted by the summary of roles and responsibilities in this chapter. From the family's perspective it may be reassuring to have so much support available, but another scenario is that it could result in 'help fatigue', which 'can sometimes make parents appear to withdraw from services' (Early Support, 2012, p. 33). The keyworker role has been developed to mitigate these circumstances through one professional taking responsibility for being the single point of contact for the family. The idea is that:

> having one individual to communicate with the family keeps the family 'on the radar' and that by working at the parents' pace families can be encouraged to re-engage and even take on things that they would not have previously considered.
>
> (Early Support, 2012, p. 33)

The keyworker role was developed as part of the Early Support Programme in England from 2003, which aimed to establish a more integrated and collaborative approach between services supporting very young disabled children (see Chapter 2). A similar programme was put in place by the Welsh government in 2011. The functions of a keyworker are summarised in Table 3.5.

Some professionals will be employed solely as keyworkers, their primary role being to provide this support for a specific number of families. These practitioners

Table 3.5 The role of the keyworker

Emotional and practical support	Providing emotional and practical support as part of a trusting relationship. Enabling and empowering the child, young person and their family to make decisions and use their personalised budgets in a way that is most effective
Coordination	Being a single point of regular and consistent contact for the child, young person and family. Facilitating multi-agency meetings. Coordinating services and practitioners around the child, young person and family.
Planning and assessment	Supporting a single planning and joint assessment process. Identifying the strengths and needs of all family members.
Information and specialist support	Providing information and signposting where necessary. Advocating on the child's, young person's and/or family's behalf where appropriate. Facilitating clinical care to be integrated with specialist and universal services.

Source: adapted from Early Support, 2012, p. 7.

are often known as 'designated' keyworkers. In other circumstances, people will take on key working responsibilities for families that they are involved with in another capacity. For example, a family's health visitor or Portage home visitor may also be their keyworker. This is known as the 'non-designated' approach. Within these arrangements the practitioner may have key working as an element of their job description, but they will generally carry out this role for far fewer families than a 'designated' keyworker.

Different localities in England have taken diverse approaches to providing key working arrangements. In some areas a key working team of designated keyworkers managed by a co-ordinator exists. In other authorities a keyworker co-ordinator will be responsible for training, supporting and supervising non-designated keyworkers in their additional responsibilities. Some areas do not have a specific co-ordinator in place, but the key working role is integrated into the responsibilities of a range of staff working with young disabled children and their families.

There are advantages and disadvantages to these various ways of organising key working. The successful development of effective non-designated keyworkers depends on the commitment of their primary agency to this approach. Commitment is demonstrated by allocating time in the practitioner's schedule to accommodate their key working activities. Because this inevitably means a reduction in the number of families they can support in their primary role, the non-designated approach can have widespread resource implications. Conversely, setting up a designated key working service can create another group of professionals for families to interact with and another set of roles and responsibilities for them to try to understand and accommodate into their daily lives. Despite these complications, by 2012 the government in England was making policy commitments to extend key working beyond the early years to young people of school age identified with SEN (DfE, 2012a). The keyworker seems set to emerge as having a long-term central role in the collaborative approach to supporting families.

Summary: formal and informal support

This chapter illustrates the wide range of different people that may be involved with a child and her family. While some of these roles are distinct, many overlap. This needs to be seen as a positive rather than a potential source of confusion – but will only be advantageous if people communicate and work closely with each other. This is particularly crucial when any planning takes place. Joint decisions between parents and professionals about who is doing what to support the child, the family and a setting must be a first step.

Professionals need to be aware of the demands they place on families in terms of the vast number of appointments they are expected to keep. This may not only be exhausting for parents and children, but may disconnect them from the potential of informal support within their own community. Both child and family can face the prospect of exclusion and disconnection as they become enclosed within their 'specialised', separate routine.

Everyone needs to be aware that professional services are not the only source of support for young children and their parents. The nuclear and extended family, as well as friends within the community, are key harbours of informal support (Dolan *et al.*, 2006). Often, such support is regarded as preferential by families because it is non-stigmatising, focused on the practical, not tied to working hours, more personal, more empathic, more durable and able to be reciprocated by returning the help at a later date (Dolan and McGrath, 2006). Although the role of the professional cannot replicate the strength and depth of these informal networks, they can aim to reflect some of these qualities in their own services. Practitioners can explore how any stigma attached to using their service can be reduced. There should be a focus on providing concrete, practical support and flexibility to meet the family's needs rather than users adjusting to meet the requirements of professionals.

Case study: Rachel McMillan Nursery School and Children's Centre

Rachel McMillan Nursery School is a maintained nursery school providing early years education and integrated childcare for babies, toddlers and children up to five years old. It offers full-time and part-time placements for over 150 three and four year olds, as well as places for over 20 children who are under three. The school has been an established part of the local community since 1914, when the child health pioneers Margaret and Rachel McMillan established the first 'open-air' nursery as the beginning of what was to become an international movement in early years education. Since 2006 the setting has also been a Sure Start Children's Centre, functioning as a hub for a variety of family support provision.

The setting considers itself to be an 'inner city school' which is 'lucky to have children of families that originate from over 30 different countries' within the nursery. This means that around 30 per cent of the children speak English as an additional language. It is also significant that around 15 per cent of the young people in the nursery are identified with SEN.

The principles of inclusion and partnership are firmly embedded within the policy and practice at Rachel McMillan. The head teacher is in no doubt that a fundamental part of developing community-focused provision is 'about valuing people, about valuing that everyone has something to offer and recognising that you don't know everything yourself, you need to work together'. Such a clear commitment to welcoming and listening to everyone from the community is evident in the nursery's 'Inclusion Statement':

* We believe that all children have the right to learn and play together.
* We celebrate the many abilities, cultures, backgrounds, differences, languages and faiths of all our children, families and staff.
* We are committed to countering discrimination in all its forms.

The positive, welcoming ethos of Rachel McMillan Nursery is tangible both for children and their families. The excellence lies not only in the high level of skill and innovatory practice, but in the warmth and understanding that underpins all activities and developments. Open, accessible drop-in services are central to the ethos of the nursery and Children's Centre. The deputy head says that it is of great value to families when they can just come in and talk to the person they want to see. The emphasis is also very much on developing a community around the nursery, with frequent sessions for parents and children to meet informally and make social connections.

Parents and carers work in partnership with the staff to ensure that their child gets the most out of the nursery day. There are regular 'stay and play' sessions where parents and staff can share ideas while engaged in activities together with the children. Parents are also at the centre of discussions with the nursery staff during times of transition. This can be: before children start at the setting; when planning is taking place to move on to primary school; and to prepare for changes within the nursery itself, such as when moving from provision for the under-threes to the nursery school classes. For children identified with SEN such preparation is tailored even more carefully around

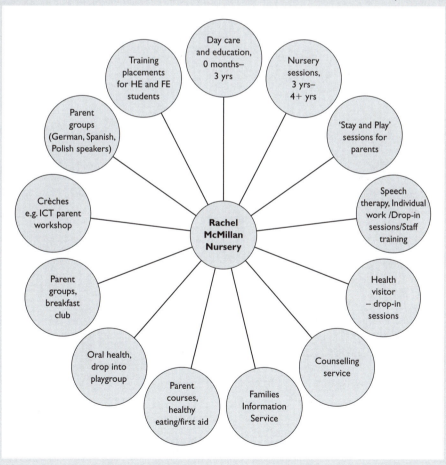

the individual, with an emphasis on liaison and collaborative working with any other services involved, such as Portage. TAC meetings are regularly held within the setting, drawing together any professionals involved and the nursery staff to plan jointly with families.

The diagram on p. 45 highlights some of the constellation of sessions, groups and services provided at Rachel McMillan. Like many other settings at the forefront of developing support for young children and their families, this nursery and Children's Centre fulfils a multi-functional role for its community. The breadth of the provision on offer reflects the complex, interwoven themes of government policy in recent times and shows us what such ideas can look like in action.

Chapter 4

Early identification and communication with parents and carers

This chapter has three sections. The first two discuss different ways in which children's early difficulties may be identified in early years settings and the implications this has for approaches to parents. The third section looks at some specific issues involved in establishing good communication with families.

SEN identified by teachers and early years practitioners

When a teacher or early years practitioner begins to have some concerns about a child and how they are getting on in school, they may wonder if they are right to be worried. Alternatively, they may feel surprised or even angry that 'no-one has picked this up before', especially when the difficulties are more apparent. Despite regular developmental checks that are now in place, some children may still fall through the net.

Clarifying concerns

The first thing is not to jump to conclusions about a child or act too hastily. Although early intervention is desirable, there is no point in intervening, perhaps inappropriately, before there is some clarity about what is needed. Observing the child in different situations over a few weeks and presenting a variety of activities to see how he approaches them will give a lot of information. Watching interactions with other children, seeing how he communicates, the level and complexity of play and doing things with him will give a much better idea of what the child can actually achieve with and without help. It will also identify more precisely the nature of his needs. If a notebook is kept somewhere accessible it is easy to jot down observations and comments without this being an arduous additional responsibility. Over time these brief entries will provide a wealth of information on which to base discussions about the child's needs with parents, colleagues and other professionals.

Avoid a 'deficit model'

It is possible to imagine a notebook containing numerous entries saying things like: *'Patrick sat doing nothing all morning'* or *'Ayse can't put her coat on by herself'*. This may all be true, but does not say anything that helps to inform future action. If an entry reads: *'Patrick was seated at the sand tray and watched other children play with the sand'*, you know something about the context he was in and about his learning. If it also said: *'When I sat with him to build a sandcastle he watched me. He was unresponsive to sentences but responsive to single words and gestures. He laughed as we knocked the sandcastle down together'*, you know how he responded to adult intervention and have some idea about the level of his receptive language. Similarly: *'Ayse can bring her coat to an adult and can put her arms in the sleeves if the coat is held'*, lets you know that she is aware of what to do, can follow a routine and has the physical ability to manage that activity. It is much more useful to think about a child as able to concentrate on a favourite activity for two minutes than to say that he cannot settle to anything at all. It facilitates more constructive communication with parents and others, and also provides a starting point from which to aim for realistic targets.

The learning and behaviour overlap

Although early concerns are often raised as a result of 'hard to manage' behaviour, this is frequently an integral part of other difficulties. Thinking about behaviour within a special needs framework helps those working with the child to maintain an appropriate professional perspective rather than taking the difficulties personally and feeling de-skilled. Clarifying behaviours for cooperation, independence, attention and play will help to discover whether:

- the child is showing immaturity in most aspects of his development and his behaviour overall is more like that of a younger child;
- the child needs more physical outlets for his level of energy;
- frustration with communication difficulties is a major cause of his behaviour;
- the child appears emotionally distressed and reacts strongly to perceived slights and/or is often angry or tearful;
- the child needs positive reinforcement to learn the behaviour required in school or pre-school settings – he will especially need to learn that he will get attention by behaving in cooperative ways;
- there is a more specific difficulty indicated by 'clusters' of behaviours.

It is easy to quickly attribute behaviour difficulties to poor parenting skills, but as can be seen from the above there are many reasons that a child might present challenges in a busy classroom. Where parents do have more limited skills or are not coping well, they need support, not condemnation. In most cases parents want the best for their child and do the best they can with the knowledge, skills, resources and support available (Roffey, 2002, 2004). Expectations for the child may need to be changed.

Taking time to accept that a child has a special need

If the child's development is noticeably delayed in one or more areas, the chances are that routine checks will have already identified this and the doctor or health visitor tried to address concerns with the child's parents. They may, however, have actively resisted the notion that their child was not progressing along the usual developmental path, and refused further investigation or intervention. This denial is not uncommon in the first instance.

Some families, perhaps those for whom English is an additional language, may find engaging with health professionals difficult or confusing if this is not supported. Others may have had little experience of other children and so little basis for comparison. Finding that there is a concern about their child may come as a shock for these families.

Other families recognise that all is not well but prefer a 'wait and see' approach.

When referrals and/or appointments are made without full parental support, the family may simply not attend. Their reluctance may stem from having experienced a lack of sensitivity and feeling blamed or guilty, as well as struggling to accept their child's difficulties.

Unless there are child protection concerns, professionals must wait until parents themselves request help for their child. It is useful to maintain a dialogue with the family, however, and hope to facilitate acceptance of the child's needs over time. This will be more likely to be fruitful if everyone is non-judgemental and supports the child and family to the best of their ability in the meantime.

Reasons for denial

When parents have little experience of young children, they may find it hard to both realise and accept that their child is different in some way from others of the same age. In some families, there sadly continues to be a stigma in having a child with difficulties, and a lot of effort may be put into not acknowledging the existence of problems, especially within the wider family network. This may also be the parents' way of handling their feelings of grief, guilt and even shame.

It may be easier for families to accept difficulties when these are more obvious and visible. Children who have communication and/or social difficulties may have experienced excellent development in most areas until they are about two years old, when the difficulties begin to become more apparent. This not only makes it harder for parents to accept there is something unusual about the way their child interacts, but also makes others less understanding and even condemnatory, particularly about any associated behaviour difficulties.

Sometimes a child has skills in one area that may be quite advanced: this can obscure other difficulties.

Parents may acknowledge that their child has difficulties but be reluctant to discuss them for fear that their child will be 'labelled'. They may worry that negative things will be written about him, that these will go on his file, that this will affect how he is seen by others now and in the future and that this may limit his opportunities. It may help to establish partnership with parents if they are initially offered informal unrecorded meetings to discuss their child's needs. When these are positive and action-focused, parents may be reassured. This model of partnership, particularly if provided at home, is the basis of much early intervention through Portage or the Early Support programme.

Messages parents receive about their child's special needs

The language that is used by professionals is vital in helping parents adjust to their child's needs. Words like 'handicapped' and 'backward' are alarming and no longer exist within the special educator's vocabulary in the UK. Difficulties are usually described in terms of the child's needs rather than in deficit terms. Despite efforts to ensure that everyone is aware of respectful terminology, not all professionals have had equal access to training, nor are they always knowledgeable about the possibilities of inclusion. Doctors may, with the best of intentions, give the impression that a child will not 'cope' in a mainstream school when, in fact, this may be entirely possible. Parents may then not always be fully open about their child's needs when they go to register him for a school place, for fear of rejection. This highlights the value of interdisciplinary working to ensure common language and understanding of expectations.

The early experiences that parents have in discussing their child's needs can make a difference in how they perceive their child, their child's education and the possibilities for future collaboration with other professionals.

One of the phrases that has been in common parlance, by special educators as well as the medical professionals, is 'developmental delay'. This means that a child has a difficulty, which may be long term. The word 'delay', however, can be very misleading for those who are not familiar with this specific usage. Delay suggests 'catching up' and sometimes this is what parents and even teachers will be seeking – the time when the child is at the same level as everyone else. Children who are developmentally delayed certainly make progress, but at their own pace. Looking for an intervention or a level of support which will reduce the gap between their skills and those of other children may be inappropriate and lead to disappointment. The focus must be on seeking optimum progress for each child, and celebrating their incremental successes and what they *can* do.

The child entering school or early years setting

When the child enters nursery or school, far from 'nothing having been done' there may, in fact, be a lot of history concerning the child's developmental needs. This makes it even more important how the child's needs are raised with parents. Giving them lots of facts about how the child is not managing will only serve to reinforce their fears and anxieties, and this may make if hard for them to 'hear' what is being said about their child's needs and what might be done to meet them.

Approaching parents in the first instance

There are no hard and fast rules as every family is different, but the following format should help early years practitioners or teachers think through their communication with parents/carers, whether there is a significant difficulty or a more minor concern. The checks that have taken place for most children will have identified anything major – unless the child has missed these.

Ask to have an informal discussion – perhaps a word at the end of a session. 'Have you got a minute – there's something I would like to ask you?' is better than immediately saying you are worried.

Start the conversation by saying something positive about the child. This is important for several reasons:

- It shows the parent that you are relating to the whole child, not just in terms of his difficulties.
- It relieves their anxieties that the child will immediately be 'labelled' or, even worse, 'excluded'.
- It shows some commitment to the child and that you are not only concerned about management.
- Once the parent's attention is secured there is more likelihood that the rest of the conversation will be heard.

Ask the parents if they have any concerns about their child's learning.

If they say they do not, you could be more specific, such as: 'I've noticed that J. seems to need/be struggling with/isn't always able to ... what happens at home?'

You could then say something like 'I'd expect most children of this age to be doing ... it looks like he needs a bit more help to get there.' If the parents continue to resist acknowledging the difficulty you could ask them if it is all right if you just kept an eye on the child and see how he gets on for a few weeks. Few parents could object to this – it is not so different from what would be happening anyway. You then have the opportunity to set up a review meeting.

If the parents are able to say that they also have concerns you may be able to talk more fully about what these are – take your lead from the parent, this may be a very difficult interaction for them. You could ask if anyone else has mentioned problems to them. If it is appropriate, you may feel able to ask the parent if you could have their permission to contact their health visitor or other involved professional for information. It will be necessary to get this permission in writing, especially for any medical information. Some parents may, in fact, be quite relieved that their own nagging worries about their child's progress are being clarified. They may welcome the opportunity to share their concerns and be pleased to know that something is being done.

It is a good idea to end the meeting with a plan of action, even if it is simply gathering more information and finding out more about how the child is doing in specific situations or putting in a minor intervention such as having the child sit close to an adult at carpet time.

A review meeting a few weeks later will ascertain whether there is a concern that requires more substantive assessment or support. At this meeting you could ask how the parents feel their child is getting along, what they think his strengths are, as well as the difficulties he seems to be experiencing.

Moving on

If it is agreed that the child's needs do require further intervention, then an IEP is drawn up. This comes under the heading of Early Years Action. The lead practitioner discusses the child with the SENCO or Inclusion Co-ordinator, who will also meet with the family to decide what might be done to help their child.

Although partnership with parents is a cornerstone of special needs legislation, and should be promoted wherever possible, it is not necessary to get parents' permission to put support programmes in place where they only involve staff who work within the setting. Parents should, however, always be informed of what is happening for their child in school. Permission will be needed if other agencies become directly involved, a stage that has been referred to as Early Years Plus. Agencies can, however, give general advice on management for the particular difficulty a child is presenting. This consultative approach is a valuable use of time for professionals as it enables their expertise to be disseminated beyond the individual to a systems level. This enhances the knowledge and skills of practitioners, who can then apply these with increased confidence in their interaction with children who have similar needs. Many services are pleased to also provide formal professional development for early years practitioners.

Regular formal reviews of the support that has been put in place will help clarify strategies that promote progress for the child. These should be regularly shared with parents so they continue to hear positive things about their child. Paradoxically, this may help them, in time, to accept the difficulties and work in partnership with the school and others. At this point parents may agree to referrals that will access the services of other appropriate professionals.

It is helpful if staff in a school or early years setting have written information about services, which they can give to parents to reassure them about what to expect. Educational psychologists and other professionals who visit early years provision regularly would see it as part of their role to meet with parents to explain what they do, and answer any queries. Parents may be reassured by this meeting and feel more comfortable about the professional's involvement with their child.

SEN identified by parents

The previous section looked at concerns that were predominantly practitioner led, and the interaction between parents and early years professionals focused on developing positive communication so that full collaboration could eventually take place.

This section is about concerns that are predominantly parent led, where parents are anxious that their child is not making sufficient progress and want their concerns to be taken seriously. In their interactions with staff, parents naturally want their views to be respected. Even if staff in the setting do not share the same initial concerns, they need to think about developing a framework in which useful home–school communication can take place.

It can be the case that a parent is the first one to notice that their child is struggling. They may be alerted to this by:

- comparisons with other children;
- the child not being able to settle and concentrate on learning tasks;
- the child not being able to do the work that is sent home;
- the child being unhappy in pre-school or school;
- the child's behaviour becoming difficult to manage.

The foundation stage curriculum

Parents may have expectations of what their child should be doing and learning which may not always be appropriate. This may be because they have an idea of what 'school is for' even if their child is only three years old. The focus on the importance of early years education may be contributing to parents' anxieties about the development of their child's skills. Where schools and nurseries take the trouble to show parents the educational value of the activities that are on offer, this can be reassuring. Parents may not realise the many ways small children learn and the vital importance of play and self-directed activity, as well as guidance to develop basic skills. Close communication with parents, not only about what takes place in the classroom but the rationale behind the activities, will also empower parents to support their child's learning at home.

Expressing a concern

Parents expressing a concern may do this in several ways. Sometimes it may be hard to get to the root of what they are trying to say. This could be for many reasons:

- They do not have the same terminology or even the same language as the teacher.
- They are anxious, or do not want to appear pushy and are hesitant.
- They fear they might be blamed for the child's 'failure to thrive'.
- They are unsure whether they should be worried or not.
- They tend to adopt a certain manner when dealing with anyone they perceive is in authority – this may range from demanding their rights to being very 'respectful'.
- The worry they have is complex and they don't know where to begin.
- Although anxieties are being expressed about their child in nursery or school, there are other worries about what is happening at home.
- They have experienced a difficult time at school themselves or they have had negative experiences with older children and perhaps feel they have to make a fuss to be heard.

Sometimes parents may start off with a mild expression of concern and become increasingly outspoken if they do not see anything happening as a result.

Practitioners might feel there is an attack on their competency. Although it is hard to see through a negative approach, it is useful, at least in the first instance, to try to focus on the anxieties being expressed about the child. If parents feel someone is really listening to them they may be reassured that their concerns are not being ignored and a more useful dialogue may ensue.

Listening

Parents have a right to express concerns, and it may be useful to give written as well as verbal information about when staff are available for a private discussion. It is more likely that parents will mention their concerns in passing and teachers can then offer to meet with them to talk it through properly.

The process of this discussion is important. It needs to be as free from interruptions as possible. A notice on the door and the phone switched off helps. Checking out how long people can stay ensures that time is left to plan what to do.

Parents need to be put at their ease and encouraged to talk. Questions that are fairly open-ended will usually elicit information, but if the parents are having difficulty expressing themselves then more closed questions may help them out:

- 'What has been bothering you?'
- 'How long have you been worried about him?'

It is not a good idea to interrupt parents at this stage to tell them that everything is all right in school – it may be perceived as dismissive. It is better to prompt in order to find out as much as possible about why the parent is worried. The focus of the concern may change as the story unfolds.

Even if the teacher truly believes that the child is progressing well, parents may not feel that their concerns have been acknowledged unless there is some action from the meeting. Alternatively, parents may very well have identified a difficulty of which the teacher had been unaware. This meeting could conclude with one or more of several options:

- Keep an eye on him for a few weeks and have another meeting.
- Find out more about the concerns expressed.
- Contact other professionals who may have been involved.
- Devise a home school programme to address some of the concerns.

It is helpful to make sure the parents have a copy of the setting or school's policy for special needs and disability so that it becomes a point of joint reference for future decisions.

Whatever the agreements, a review date should be set. At this point it may be appropriate to initiate Early Years Action and develop an IEP for the child.

'How well does your partnership policy work in practice?'

Finding out

If the child is in a pre-school provision, initial information can be gained by working through the Two Year Progress Check or looking at his progress against early learning goals. Likewise, if he is in infant school, the Foundation Stage Profile may be useful.

In infant school, parents may be particularly worried about their child getting to grips with literacy. It would be wise to check out some pre-reading skills to identify any underlying problems with eyesight or hearing, especially finer skills such as visual and auditory discrimination. Can the child identify rhyme? Can he see small differences between pictures and symbols? Checking early language development and any family history will also give an indication as to the likelihood of literacy difficulties arising.

Teachers may like further guidance about what might be involved in difficulties with early reading processes, what to look for and how to go about it. A first step after consultation with the SENCO might be to ask an advisory teacher or the EP. Most services would be pleased to do this and do not require the referral of an individual child.

Emotional development and learning

It may be that the child is not progressing as well as he might because of an emotional difficulty. Worries about things at home, bullying by other children, anxiety about getting things wrong may all be contributory factors. Asking parents if any of these factors could be present is the first step.

Parents are often unaware of the links between emotional development and learning. Family breakdown or bereavement is often not discussed with small children, who suddenly find themselves without a significant person in their lives. They may be very confused, think it must be their fault, need a great deal of reassurance, have poor concentration or become angry and badly behaved. It is common for children's attainments in school to suffer as a consequence, or for them to be unsettled or unhappy in their setting, giving already distressed parents something else to worry about.

These issues may be very difficult for parents to talk about unless they have a particularly close relationship with the teacher or key member of staff. Having some general guidance available may therefore be helpful (see Dowling and Elliott, 2012). Again, the EP service is a useful contact for advice on these issues.

Moving on

It may be that the picture changes as a result of early investigations. Further tests of hearing, vision or other referrals may be indicated.

It may be appropriate to organise further levels of support or assessment within the process of the SEN Code of Practice.

If the child is in school, parents who have raised the concern themselves are usually willing to be part of a home school programme. It is likely that such programmes are already in place to some extent for all the children in the class. A more specific one for the child in question might be appropriate under the following conditions:

- It provides opportunities for the child to receive positive attention at home.
- It aims at reinforcing learning rather than introducing new concepts.
- It is enjoyable and not stressful for either parent or child.
- It is not onerous for the parent, who may have problems fitting it into a busy schedule.
- It helps parents understand their child's learning better.

Negotiating what is possible for the parents, what is needed for the child to maintain motivation and how the programme will be reviewed are all necessary components of a successful home school intervention. For children in the pre-school years, practitioners in settings may work alongside the Portage service or early years specialist teachers who may be supporting children's learning at home.

Seeking resources

It may be that the parents want individual support for their child and will come to meetings with the view that they need to 'fight for their child'. Following the listening suggestions above is the first step. Explaining carefully the policy on SEN and ways in which assessments are carried out and linked to a plan–do–review cycle of intervention may also help. It is not useful to talk to parents about the needs of other children or the stresses on teachers or staff – it is their child who matters to them.

Good communication means close involvement with parents who can see what is being done, and are part of the solution. Once it is clear their concerns are being taken seriously, initial assessments and investigations being carried out and plans put into place, most will be reassured.

A very few parents, however, will see their child as being held back by the provision on offer, which they do not see as addressing his specific difficulties. They may want resources that are not available for their child's level of need and be less than responsive to a considered approach. There is no easy answer to this except to:

- acknowledge their natural concerns in wanting the best for their child;
- be very clear how early years policy links to the legislation and guidance on SEN;
- share the information on which decisions are made;
- provide information about what is done in the class to promote skills;
- give information about support groups;
- talk about activities or make reference to books or programmes which may support and extend their child's learning at home;
- keep open the lines of communication wherever possible;
- provide regular information about the child's achievements and progress in all aspects of the curriculum;
- link attainments with the wellbeing and development of the whole child;
- think about the time issues involved and make appointments to see the parents which have a structure, a beginning and an end.

Specific issues in communicating with parents/carers

Language and cultural issues

Communication and collaboration with many families is affected by cultural and language issues. This is not simply addressed by having access to interpreting and translation services, although that is better than nothing. Families from different ethnic backgrounds, especially if they are more recent arrivals to the UK, may have very little understanding of the educational context, let alone all the processes and terminology surrounding special needs and disability. Some local authorities and schools have made videos showing what goes on in schools, pre-school settings and Children's Development Centres and have provided commentaries in community languages.

In some cultures, having a disabled child has different or additional meanings to those that might be expected. The level of shame, for instance, might be shocking to those with a Western ideology and it could be easy to be judgemental about this. Working with local communities and encouraging a two-way exchange of information is useful. Where possible, translations of materials and information should be done in conjunction with people from local communities. It is easy to make cultural errors even if the translated language is correct.

For strict Muslim families, it is not acceptable for a woman to be in the presence of a man other than her husband unless he is present. This may present difficulties in setting up effective home–school communication and may mean that some families require a more flexible approach.

Communication with both parents

Under the Children Act, both parents have rights and responsibilities, even if they are not living together. This only applies to parents who were married at the time of the child's birth. Unmarried fathers have to get the court's or the mother's agreement to gain parental responsibility. Education legislation defines a parent as anyone who has this parental responsibility or is looking after the child; there is no obligation on schools to release information to anyone without such parental responsibility.

In many cases when we talk about parents we are referring to one person, usually the mother. It is often valuable, however, to encourage the active participation of both parents, including step-parents and other partners, who may be of the same or different gender. Sometimes this may mean flexibility in service delivery, perhaps to see the family in the evening and/or at home or together on neutral territory. The reasons for promoting a joint approach are not always obvious, but are nevertheless important. Having a child with SEN puts both individuals and families under pressure. Lack of mutual support and understanding can exacerbate the stresses, to the detriment of everyone. When both parents or other family members are actively involved:

- it enables the responsibilities to be shared;
- information is less likely to get distorted;
- it promotes appropriate expectations;

- it helps parents to come to terms with the difficult feelings they may be experiencing;
- it can point both parents to sources of information and support;
- it helps to maintains a positive relationship for the child with both parents;
- it promotes consistency of care for the child.

It is not always easy, nor always appropriate, to actively involve both parents, but where it is not going to be disadvantageous to the child it is worth considering how to promote a joint approach.

Although confidential information can only be shared with parents unless they give their permission for it to be shared with others, it can often help to engage members from both sides of the extended family, especially grandparents. This can increase both practical and emotional support without placing demands for help on a very small number. Single parents, in particular, may also be given the choice to invite a close friend for support.

Looked after children

Some children, for many reasons, are not living with either of their natural parents. For children with disabilities and SEN this is more likely to be the case than in the rest of the population. For such children, communication may need to be maintained with several adults.

'Looked after' children are either 'accommodated' or are the subject of a Care Order. The first is a voluntary arrangement between parents and the local authority Children's Services and is usually the outcome of a request for help. Parents must have the opportunity to be involved in all meetings and decisions about their child.

Where there has been a Care Order made by a Family Court, the local authority share parental responsibility with the parents, whether the child is living at home or not. There will be a social worker responsible for the child's welfare; this is the person who should be approached to discuss permission for referrals. He or she should be invited to all major reviews and should ensure that education is represented at any case conferences arranged by the Children's Services department. The social worker will be able to give information about the continuing rights and responsibilities of the child's natural parents and what is appropriate communication with them.

The child may be cared for in a foster family, sometimes in a small residential children's home or increasingly with family members – such as grandparents. If the child is in residential care, it is helpful to establish a close relationship with the key-worker, who can then communicate with other staff in the home. Foster carers may be looking after children on a temporary or more long-term basis. Although they do not have any legal parental responsibility they do take the parental role for children on day-to-day matters and communication needs to be maintained with them in the same way as with other parents.

In cases where a Family Court is making decisions about the care of children, a 'Children's Guardian' is appointed. This person is responsible for ensuring that the child is represented independently in the decision-making process and will prepare a report for the court about the child's needs, wishes and feelings.

Summary

Partnership with parents requires professionals to be non-judgemental, have a high level of sensitivity and pay attention to processes as well as the content of communication. It requires not only interpersonal skills but also organisational structures and policies which ensure that good practice for SEN and the partnership between home and school, nursery or other pre-school provision is part of the whole early years ethos.

Case study: The best and the worst of experiences
The story of Max and his family

Max is now seven years old. He is a lively and loving little boy who chats non-stop. He can write his name, do gym, is beginning to read and make connections with meaning.

But to get him to this stage, where he is making optimal progress, has been a long, hard and often bumpy road.

Max was born at 27 weeks and weighed less than two pounds. There was no indication that anything was seriously wrong until he had a routine neonate brain scan at around two months. Doctors took his parents aside and announced that Max had hemi-megalencephaly and would be likely to have epilepsy. 'Then, they just said goodbye', says Max's mother, Bini. Nothing was offered except routine check-ups.

Everything changed at 15 months when Max was referred to Portage by the consultant paediatrician because his upper and lower limbs were not developing at the same rate. Bini says it was the best thing that could have happened – someone to support the family and provide a source of information and comfort. The Portage worker came once each week to work with Max and the family, helped manage appointments, fill in forms and was able to refer to speech and language therapy and hydrotherapy – all based at Cricket Green polyclinic. Max turned out not to be epileptic, but he did have a range of other needs, including fine motor skills, language, hearing and vision. At Cricket Green there would be regular meetings chaired by the consultant paediatrician, where everyone involved with Max came and said what they were pleased about and what help he needed. Bini felt fully involved and Max thrived. He loved the interventions and made progress. Little and often was the way to go.

It was when Max began to attend nursery school at three years that everything went wrong. Although the Portage worker provided an IEP for the transition, physiotherapy, OT and hydrotherapy all disappeared. When Max started in education he was allowed four half-hour sessions for speech and language every quarter and this was never at the same place or with the same person. The structure of his mouth made it difficult for him to articulate words and he became frustrated at not being understood. It also isolated him from other children. This experience made Bini determined to fight for her son's needs. When Max was four he began at his local primary school with a lunchtime supervisor. By then he had a Statement of Special Educational Needs, but according to Bini it didn't specify what her son needed at all. Despite the considerable expense, the family decided to go to tribunal. The tribunal was adjourned for reports, which doubled the cost and puts such a move out of the reach of many parents.

In the meantime Max was referred to Great Ormond Street Hospital (GOSH) for Children. It was their report of his complex needs, together with a diagnosis of Proteus Syndrome, that swung the balance. Max now attends Blossom House in south London, where he is doing well. This special school has a solution-focused approach with pupils – if one thing doesn't work they try another. The children have a range of needs, but learn from each other's strengths. Max has friends there. Bini says she has a huge sense of partnership both with the school and also with GOSH, where she can make contact by phone or email whenever there is a problem. But it is for Portage that she reserves the greatest accolade: 'If anyone has the most humanity in them it is the Portage Association.'

Chapter 5

Joint planning for identified needs

Children who have significant difficulties in one or more areas of their development and have had assessments and probably a home intervention programme may enter early years education with a good level of information about their current SEN. For most children there will be a continuing need for ongoing assessment to help clarify the best way forward. Small children develop quickly and continual assessment and monitoring is important for all children in the early years.

Some children with a high level of complex and/or severe needs may begin their schooling in special provision. A number of these children may stay in a segregated setting throughout their school life. Other children may find themselves in a nursery or Children's Centre where there is a high level of staff expertise contributing to ongoing assessment. Increasingly, however, parents are seeking a mainstream provision for their children where they can play and learn alongside their peers. This is especially so in the early years.

There is a balance to be had between intensive early specialist provision, which may give children skills to enhance their longer-term inclusion, and opportunities to learn and play alongside peers who attend their local mainstream setting. What is agreed, however, is that all staff should have a good knowledge of the child's needs that enables appropriate approaches and expectations to be made.

Although the law now says very clearly that admission policies must not discriminate against children with SEN, there is still the 'conditional' clause that refers to the impact on other children. The response parents receive when they approach a school or nursery may not therefore be predictably favourable. It will depend on the ethos and value system of the setting, the organisational structure and the level of confidence that staff have in being able to meet the child's needs. In some schools and early years settings, normal functioning is stressed and any special or additional needs are taken in their stride. Where mainstream provision is less than welcoming there may be a fear that the child will take up a disproportionate amount of time and attention, and that support services will not be available. In some hard-pressed local authorities resources are certainly stretched to the limit, but even here some early years settings and schools are much more accepting than others, and prepared to develop their knowledge, skills and structures to meet the needs of all their pupils as individuals. Inclusive education is a process, both for the child and for the school or pre-school. There are always improvements to be made, whatever the starting point.

Case study: Lanterns Nursery School and Children's Centre
A network of support for children with SEN

Lanterns is an inclusive nursery school and Children's Centre providing for around 80 children from the local community in Winchester, alongside 30–40 children identified with SEN. Children in this group are referred from a range of professionals. The children who take up the referral places at the nursery are often familiar with the surroundings, having attended one of the Centre's groups specifically for young children with SEN.

Early Start

This is a physiotherapy-based group for children under two and their parents. The aim of each weekly session is to develop motor and communication skills through music and action games. A physiotherapist attends to provide advice and support for parents, and other professionals may also join the sessions.

Smart Start

This is a weekly group for children aged between two and three, which supports early communication and motor skill development. The group is facilitated by the early support co-ordinator based in the centre. Professionals from SLT, OT and physiotherapy visit the sessions. Parents stay with their child during the group, working with the appropriate therapist on recommended next steps. Such focused activities are integrated into the play and social routine within the room. Significantly, the environment is set up to replicate a room in the main nursery, e.g. a mark-making area; a book corner; a playdough and role-play section. During the sessions Makaton songs and signs used in the main nursery are introduced, as well as visual symbols and timetables. This supports transition for those children that move into the nursery school around their third birthday.

A number of other assessment, outreach and support services run from the centre to maximise its provision for children and families. These include the following.

LEAP (Lanterns Early Assessment Programme)

This group has been set up for children between two and three years of age for whom there is concern about development. It is run by experienced early years practitioners working as an integrated team, including the community nursery nurse, family support outreach worker, senior early years practitioner and communication and language assistant. Parents attend with their children for five weekly sessions in a relaxed play environment in which their child's needs can be assessed and discussed. Further guidance can be provided to families at the end of the programme and referrals on to other support considered.

Lanterns Early Years Outreach Service

This service is provided to pre-schools and Year R classes to support provision for children with special needs or behavioural difficulties. Referrals are made via the area inclusion co-ordinators, who have direct contact with pre-school settings. Following referral, the Outreach Service visits to discuss issues with the staff, observe the situation and perhaps work directly with the child in the context of their play environment. The aim is to develop an agreed action plan for all involved. Subsequent visits are arranged to review progress depending on the requirements of the child and the group. The Outreach Service also provides support for children transferring from Lanterns Nursery to their mainstream school.

Special Start

This is a parent and baby group for families whose baby has spent time in the special care baby unit or who has recently received a diagnosis associated with disability. The group is aimed at parents with babies under six months old, and runs on a weekly basis. There are opportunities for play, baby massage and meeting with professionals from relevant services when they drop-in to the group.

Kids First

This is a family support group that meets monthly with other parents whose children have additional needs. Each meeting features a talk by a visiting professional on a relevant topic, such as toilet training, visual timetables or 'Team around the Child' (TAC) meetings.

The network of support is particularly well facilitated at Lanterns. The Portage Service, Homestart and Early Support team share a main office with the Children's Centre staff, which naturally encourages joint working and planning. The deputy head of the nursery noted 'it is so helpful having them all in one office – we can do all this in two seconds rather than thinking we will have to find where they are and can we talk to them....' The integrated approach also underpins the inclusion of children with SEN in both the main nursery sessions and the Children's Centre activities. The early support co-ordinator may first meet a child when they are a few weeks old and keep in regular contact while supporting their keyworker. From these initial connections the family and child may then be introduced to the Early Start group, and from the age of two move on to the Smart Start sessions at the centre. Transition into the main nursery around the age of three then represents the next positive step forward within a well-established network of support and provision.

Factors which support inclusive practices

The Inclusive Practice Project at Aberdeen University is mostly focused on teacher training, but this is not just concerned with what educators know and learn to do but also on the beliefs and understanding that underpin practice (Rouse, 2007). This includes a shift from the question 'what is wrong with this child?' to the more solution-focused 'what does this child need to support her learning?'. When teachers believe it is their responsibility to teach *all* children, it helps to improve their confidence in doing so when this responsibility is shared. Interestingly, teachers felt that not only did they need more professional development on aspects of SEN and disability, they also needed to learn how to work more effectively with other adults in supporting children.

The research quoted in the first edition of this book is still relevant today. Judy Sebba and Darshan Sachdev (1997) collated evaluation studies in inclusive education. Among the factors they identified as positive are:

- the quality of joint planning – especially in relation to the effective use of support in the classroom;
- descriptive educational labels rather than categorical labels, e.g. reading difficulty rather than Down syndrome;
- teachers who provide a role model for pupils in terms of their expectations and the respect and value they demonstrate for all pupils;
- strategies which raise children's skills in communicating – some children do not cue in to more subtle communications;
- teaching strategies which enable all pupils to participate and learn;
- pupil participation and learning which can be enhanced by high expectations, drawing on pupils' previous experiences and maximising peer support;
- flexible use of support which enhances rather than impedes the process of inclusive education.

Meeting the child and parents

Before any planning takes place the staff who will be most involved will have met with the child and her parents, even if only briefly. Talking about someone you know as a real person is much more meaningful than having just a name. Even if it raises anxieties about how to meet needs, it will help to specify those needs in the context of the whole child rather than as abstract concepts.

Joint planning meeting

The rest of this chapter is intended to help people think through the needs of individual children and how these can be met in the early years setting and beyond. The importance of this initial meeting in nursery or school cannot be over-emphasised for the following reasons:

- gathering and sharing all relevant information;
- enabling good-quality planning to take place to maximise learning in all domains of development;

- handing over between professionals;
- valuing the contributions that everyone make;
- establishing good communications;
- establishing positive relationships;
- promoting a positive 'can-do' ethos;
- reassuring parents;
- reassuring and supporting staff who will be in direct contact with the child;
- addressing potential difficulties early on;
- detailing the need for any specific resources from outside school/nursery.

Many parents, especially those who are on their own, appreciate being given the opportunity to bring a friend or other supporter along with them. It not only gives them more confidence, but they are able to talk over afterwards what has been said in the meeting. Parents of children with significant needs may already have a key-worker. This person may also be attached to another service, such as Portage, but may fulfil this co-ordinating function as their primary role. Families should also have been informed of any voluntary agency that may be able to support them, and given the contact details of the Independent Parental Supporter. It is a good idea to check that they do have all this information.

Professionals are likely to know each other as colleagues and need to be aware of doing anything that may make parents feel excluded. This includes discussing another matter in their hearing or using first names when the family are not offered the same option.

There will be a lot to discuss and detailed plans to be made. It is essential that enough time be given for this, although some of the basic information-gathering could be done beforehand. The agenda will need to include gathering of information, general planning, developing an IEP that identifies short-term targets for the child and dates for review.

The participants in the meeting will have the following contributions to make.
Parents will know:

- their child's history;
- their child's personality;
- what she can currently do at home and what she is just beginning to learn;
- whether she is able to settle to one activity or flits from one thing to another;
- what she particularly likes to do and/or is good at;
- what activities she is not interested in or actively resists;
- how determined, confident or dependent she is;
- the experiences she has already had and her responses to these experiences;
- what encourages, upsets and soothes her;
- the circumstances in which she is most and least cooperative;
- the circumstances in which she is most anxious or most confident;
- other things that influence her mood and motivation;
- how she communicates;
- how she deals with frustration;
- what they have found has worked well in supporting their child to learn.

Parents know their child best

Curious

Determined

Loving

Can't hear well from behind

There is now a greater focus on the voice of the child and how this might be elicited (Figure 5.1). Parents will be able to give their child's views about things and keyworkers will be able to add to this. Even when children do not have good language skills, they are still capable of communicating likes and dislikes, preferences and anxieties.

Parents will also know about specific circumstances at home and at work that will impinge on their own involvement. Parents may be reluctant to appear uncooperative or to divulge what they see as personal information and may therefore agree to participate in suggested actions which are they are unlikely to be able to carry through. This sets up bad feelings all round. Great care needs to be taken to ensure that decisions are made together and not imposed.

Practitioners and professionals are increasingly expected to take account of the child's wishes, elicit their opinion and empower them to contribute to decision making. For young children, especially those with a high level of need, there is uncertainty about 'how to listen' to children. The Mosaic Approach brings together verbal and visual tools specifically designed to elicit young children's perspectives.

Tools used in the Mosaic Approach

Child observation: Observers watch the child play and record a narrative account of their actions and interactions structured around two questions from the child's standpoint: 'Do you listen to me?' and 'What is it like for me to be here?' There is inevitably an adult perspective in interpretations, but observation is a good starting point.

Child interviews: These can be conducted one-to-one or in a group. Questions focus on important people, places and activities. Interviewers need to be flexible as young children who are mobile rarely stay in one place for long! This means following their lead – in time and space.

Photos and book-making: The child takes photographs of what is important to them in the setting. They choose the most important to put into their own book.

Tours: The child is asked to take the 'listening adult' on tour of the site, both indoors and outdoors. The children choose where to go and how to record the tour. This can be in the form of photos, drawing and/or sound.

Map-making: The child uses their recordings to make a map of the site and its important features.

Magic carpet: Slide show of familiar and unknown places. This activity encourages children to comment on their current environment in relation to other spaces.

Adult interviews: Informal interviews with practitioners and family members who are important in children's lives.

Processes used in the Mosaic Approach

The first stage of listening is gathering information using the methods above; the second is discussing the child's perspectives with other significant adults. This enriches understanding and is a particularly valuable aspect of the process. Thirdly, if the voice of the child is to be meaningful, then actions need to be taken as a result.

Figure 5.1 Listening to children: the Mosaic Approach (Clarke and Statham, 2005).

Parents are likely to be concerned about how happy their child will be in the pre-school setting or school, how she will settle in, how she will manage and learn, whether or not she will be able to make friends and what will happen at playtime. Many parents will be very aware of their young child's vulnerabilities and will be especially protective.

Early years teachers and educators will share some of the knowledge that is brought to the meeting by parents and other professionals. Their specific expertise, however, lies in knowledge of:

- the developmental needs of this age group;
- the educational value of play and other activities for young children;
- a range of teaching methods and approaches;
- the structure of the day and the week – what happens when;
- the EYFS curriculum that is on offer;
- what children need to carry out certain activities;
- the available resources;
- expectations for work and behaviour;
- the layout of the early years setting or school and what happens where;
- policies and procedures for a variety of issues;
- roles and responsibilities within the school or early years setting.

Teachers are likely to be concerned about helping the child make progress, whether they will have the time and resources to do this effectively, where their support is coming from, how this child's needs will affect their ability to manage the needs of the rest of the class and the expectations on them from parents and others.

EPs, inclusion advisory teachers or early years specialist teachers will know:

- about the interaction between different areas of child development;
- what is within the range of normal functioning and what gives rise to concern;
- what is needed to develop and maintain a child's confidence, self-esteem and motivation;
- factors within an organisation which help to promote communication and a positive ethos;
- factors within classrooms which enhance social interaction;
- about learning styles;
- ways of modifying the curriculum and adapting the environment;
- ways of thinking about and managing difficult behaviour;
- relevant legislation and special needs procedures;
- the range of available resources within the local authority, access procedures and criteria;
- any support groups in the locality;
- any professional development they can provide.

EPs are likely to be concerned that the child is seen as a whole person who makes progress in all domains of development. They will focus on all the interactive factors within the context of the classroom, the school and the family to ensure that these are taken into account when addressing needs. They will be particularly concerned that everyone has appropriate expectations.

Health professionals will know:

- the child's medical history and identified health-related difficulties;
- the implications these may have for learning and development;
- any other implications they may have;
- what specific health-related interventions have been undertaken and/or may be necessary;
- any specialist equipment that may be necessary;
- available resources and how to access these;
- the monitoring required;
- their own organisational structures in relation to communication with others;
- about any relevant voluntary agencies;
- what training they are able to offer.

Some health professionals, especially health visitors who will have had a more long-term relationship with the child and her family, may also have detailed know-ledge of the family's medical and social history.

Health professionals are likely to be most focused on ensuring that the child makes optimum progress in their specific area of concern. They may want to know how programmes they devise and strategies they suggest will be put in place by those in regular contact with the child. Where health workers cannot attend a meeting in person, it is helpful to request written reports from them well in advance. These should give details of their past and future involvement and outline the implications that the child's needs have for their learning. Suggestions for adaptations and/or specific interventions would also be welcome.

Children's Services may be represented if the child has an additional need, such as being the subject of a Care Order. They will be able to inform the planning meeting of issues related to the child's care and living arrangements.

Specific areas of SEN

Each of the following sections deals with a specific SEN or disability. This section is structured to assist early years staff to find out what they need to know in order to plan for the child to have an optimum pre-school and infant school experience. This means ensuring that they have access to the activities on offer and that there are frameworks in place to facilitate social inclusion.

Many children with special needs have multiple disabilities. For these children, early years professionals will want to know the answers to questions in several sections. Likewise, not all the questions in each section will be appropriate. It may be a good idea to think about what information is needed before the first planning meeting using the checklists provided.

Be precise in asking for extra help where necessary

When additional help is to be sought from the local authority, it is useful if schools or pre-schools are precise about how they are utilising their own resources and what they need in addition to these. Asking for support for specific interventions is better than simply asking for someone to be available for so many hours. One of the main criticisms of special needs support in the past has been that it is not sufficiently focused and assistants not always clear about their exact function other than 'being with' the child in question. The focus needs to be on what is necessary for the child to have access to the full learning environment.

Don't panic!

These lists of questions may look very daunting and may make a teacher or early years practitioner feel that the task of working with a child with SEN will be overwhelming. The reality is that knowledge can be quite freeing. Understanding more precisely what is required and planning how needs can be met raises confidence. Panic is more likely to set in when people are at a loss to know what to do and have to think on their feet all the time. Planning at the outset how all the adults in the class or group, as well as the other children, can be involved is a way of reducing stress.

Physical needs

This could be a difficulty with mobility, with manipulation, the processes that affect language or bodily functions such as eating or toileting. Communication and self-help skills are discussed elsewhere so this section is restricted to issues that affect mobility and manipulation. The multi-disciplinary meeting should include a physiotherapist and, where possible, an OT. Where communication or eating is an issue, a speech therapist should also be present.

Some children have a physical difficulty as the result of an accident or illness. Others will have conditions such as cerebral palsy or spina bifida. Children who have little control over their physical bodies, including their ability to communicate, may have very alert and able minds. Others may have a learning difficulty in addition to their physical disability.

It is a legal requirement that all new schools are built so all children can have access. The interventions that are planned will depend both on the answers to the questions below and the present environment and resources of the school.

Independent mobility: what you need to know

- How well he is able to move with and without assistance.
- What sort of assistance is required.
- The child's ability and willingness to communicate his need for assistance.
- Circumstances in which extra support may be required, e.g. steps, sloping or uneven surfaces.
- The child's confidence in getting around on his own.
- The sorts of things which might promote his confidence.
- Does he need additional time to get from place to place?
- Is he likely to be vulnerable in the playground or in outdoor activities? In what ways? What might make him less vulnerable?

- Are there any activities that cannot be adapted for him? What should happen at these times?
- Is any physical activity particularly stressful? What helps to make it less stressful?
- Does he get very tired at certain times? What is the best way of dealing with this? What happens at home? Would arrangements need to be made for him to have a nap during the day?
- Are there any activities that he particularly enjoys or is good at?
- If the child has a wheelchair, what help does he need to get in and out of it?
- Is there a need for special seating in the playroom or classroom? How is that arranged and what should happen when the child begins to outgrow this?
- Does he need anything else to maintain a posture that enables him to participate in tabletop or other activities.
- Does the child have difficulty maintaining his balance? What assistance does he need with this?
- Does the child have control over his movements, e.g. does he fling his arms out? What is the best way of making sure that other children can play with him but avoid flailing arms? What happens at home?
- Does the child have a particular strength/weakness in one side? What does this mean for presenting activities?
- What level of control does he have over the manipulation of objects? What helps him to manipulate things better?
- What factors in posture and physical support make a difference?
- What things does he particularly like to play with?
- Is there anything that other children need to know/do to be able to play with him?
- Does he need exercises to be carried out at the setting? How often and how long for? Who is the most appropriate person to do this?
- What training is needed for staff? Who will carry this out and when?
- Does he need any equipment? Who will monitor and maintain this?
- What interventions have taken place so far and with what outcome?
- Are there communication or self-help needs? If so, move on to the appropriate sections.

Self-help needs

Feeding, toileting and dressing are skills that small children are still developing, and not all children entering nursery or school are fully independent. It is also not uncommon for children to regress in their abilities when they have had changes or stresses in their lives. Independence skills, especially toileting, often give rise to strong opinions, feelings and potential conflict. In infant schools especially, it appears to cause busy teachers most concern and anxiety. The health visitor and/or the EP will be able to give information about these needs. If the child has difficulty eating, then the SLT can also provide advice. Parents of all children have become more protective in recent years and some are reluctant to encourage independence: this is likely to be more so where there are SEN. It is useful to help parents understand that children need to have challenges to thrive. Getting things right takes time, so neither the parent nor child should become too disheartened, nor adults 'take over' when a child makes mistakes. If tasks are presented at the right level progress will occur, if slowly.

Feeding: what you need to know

- To what extent is the child able to feed herself independently? Is she motivated to try to feed herself?
- Does she have any oral motor difficulties, i.e. can she bite, chew, suck and swallow? If so, what interventions have been in place to address this?
- Does her food have to be of a particular consistency?
- How does she get food from plate to mouth?
- What help, if any, does she need with drinks? Does this require a special cup?
- Is she independent but very messy? What can be done to alleviate this problem?
- Is she independent but very slow? Is it appropriate for extra time to be made available? How can this be arranged?
- Does the child have strong likes and dislikes for certain foods?
- Are mealtimes a source of potential conflict? What, in particular, might trigger this? What alleviates this?
- Are there medical concerns about diet, e.g. is the child failing to thrive, very listless or potentially lacking essential nutrients? Has the advice of a dietician been sought?
- Is the child allergic to any particular food? How serious is this? Is there a need for training in emergency procedures?

Toileting: what you need to know

- Does the child have a physical difficulty with his bladder or bowels that means he is unlikely ever to be clean and/or dry?
- Has the child developed skills that have since been lost? Is any possible reason for this known and is it a continuing concern?
- If the child is in nappies, how long do they stay dry/clean?
- Does the child indicate when he has soiled/wet himself? How?
- Is he distressed by having a soiled or wet nappy?
- Is he able to indicate the urge to empty his bladder or bowels? How?
- Does he have any level of control over his bladder and/or bowels, i.e. can he 'hold on' for any length of time?
- Is there any pattern to his toileting habits, e.g. needing to go 30 minutes after a meal?
- What do parents currently do at home?
- Does the child use a potty/a child-sized toilet seat?
- What encourages the child to get on and stay put?
- What is considered a reasonable time for the child to sit on a potty or toilet?
- Has there been any attempt at toilet training? What was the outcome?
- Is there a need to develop a home school programme?
- What are the child's present expectations about being changed and washed?
- What resources and facilities are available in the setting?

Dressing: what you need to know

- To what extent can the child dress/undress herself independently?
- Is she motivated to do things for herself?
- What are the expectations at home?
- Can she manage but is very slow? Is this a potential source of conflict? What alleviates/exacerbates this?
- Which circumstances in school will require the child to dress herself?
- What exactly will she need help with? Is there a need to allow extra time?
- What are the expectations on other children to help each other?
- What are the expectations to try to do things independently before asking for help?
- Is it possible to have clothes that are easier to manage, e.g. with Velcro fastenings?

Communication needs

It is estimated that as many as one in five children entering school have communication difficulties for one reason or another. Although specific programmes can be developed for individuals, a strong focus on language development for all children in the early years is essential as this underpins many other areas of development, especially thinking skills and social interaction.

The person most involved will be the SLT. If the child has a social and communication difficulty on the autistic spectrum, the EP will also need to be involved, along with any specialist advisory teacher. The child and his family may already have seen these professionals, but this is not always the case.

What you need to know

- Does the child have hearing loss? If so, please also see the section on hearing impairment.
- Are the child's skills delayed in all or most areas of development? Is his language at the same level? If so, please also see the section on learning difficulties.
- Is English the child's first language? If not, does the child have difficulties in understanding or using the language he hears at home? If the child's skills are age appropriate in their own language, then he does not have a special need in language development. Many interventions for children with language difficulties or delay are, however, also helpful for children learning an additional language.
- What is the nature of the child's difficulty with communication? Is language normal but delayed, or is it disordered in some way? Is the communication difficulty part of a wider social difficulty? Is the communication causing frustration and challenging behaviour? Ongoing assessment may be necessary to identify the child's specific difficulties.

Motivation and participation: what you need to know

- To what extent is the child motivated to communicate:
  - with adults?
  - with other children?

- Which circumstances/individuals promote this motivation?
- Which circumstances, if any, inhibit communication and need to be avoided?
- How does the child respond when others make approaches?
  - Adults?
  - Other children?
- To what extent does the child:
  - follow routines?
  - join in structured activities?
  - play meaningfully with other children?
- What would be initial steps to support the child's participation?

Receptive skills/understanding: what you need to know

- To what extent is the child able to listen?
- What are the best ways of gaining the child's attention?
  - Individually?
  - In a group?
- What is known to be useful in supporting the child's understanding?
- Has the child any knowledge of sign language? If so, which signs are in use? Are there any training implications for staff (and other children)?
- How much information can the child understand at a time? One idea or more?
- What are good ways of checking that the child has understood?

Expressive communication: what you need to know

- Does the child have a problem with:
  - saying words clearly?
  - word-finding?
  - sentence construction?
- Does the child initiate interaction with adults/other children? How do they do this? How successful are these attempts, and with what outcome? What are the best ways of responding to the child's attempts to communicate?
- How does the child communicate:
  - needs?
  - ideas?
  - feelings?
- Are there words/phrases that can be interpreted by the family but are difficult for unfamiliar people to understand? How can this knowledge be transferred?
- What, if anything, does the child use to augment verbal interaction? Does he use signs or a picture/symbol system like PECS (Picture Exchange Communication System)?
- What could be encouraged and developed?
- What would be helpful for other children to know or learn to optimise communication with this particular child?

- What affects the child's level of frustration and how is this frustration expressed? Which ways of managing this have had some success?
- Which communication targets would best help settle the child into the school or nursery?

Hearing needs

Many small children under seven years old experience conductive hearing loss at some time or another, especially when they have a cold. When a fairly severe hearing difficulty has been identified prior to school it is more likely to be a sensorineural loss, which may be permanent. Severe and/or frequent conductive loss, however, can affect a child's language and social development and needs to be taken seriously. In many cases a child with a sensorineural hearing impairment can have their residual hearing affected by an additional fluctuating conductive loss.

The audiologist and the peripatetic teacher for the hearing impaired will be able to answer many queries about a child who cannot hear well. Please also see the section above on communication difficulties.

What you need to know

- What is the nature of the child's difficulties?
- Does the child have more residual hearing in one ear? Which one?
- What sort of sounds can the child hear and at what level?
- Does the child have a history of fluctuating hearing?
- Under which circumstances is hearing worse or better?
- What does this mean for the child receiving instruction in the classroom? Where does the teacher need to be in relation to the child?
- What does this mean for less formal situations?
- How well can the child lip-read? What makes this easier?
- Is the child used to hearing aids? Are there any difficulties with these? Has the child developed any skills in managing these independently? How are hearing aids monitored?
- Does the child use any signing to support communication? If so, are there any training implications?
- Are there circumstances in which poor hearing puts the child at risk? How can these risks be addressed?
- Has the child had experience of playing with other children? What helps to make this successful?
- How well has the child adapted to these difficulties?
- What helps the child make progress?
- Are there situations or circumstances that the child finds particularly distressing? What helps?
- Which activities might need specific adaptations or arrangements, e.g. music and singing?
- What early years input has the child and family already received? What are the outcomes from this?

Visual needs

Comparatively few young children born in the UK have severe problems with their eyesight. Teachers are therefore less used to making adaptations for them than they may be, for instance, for a child with hearing loss. There are many reasons why a child has poor vision, and specific visual impairments may require different adaptations in the classroom. The peripatetic teacher for the visually impaired will be helpful in identifying appropriate responses. Some children will already be on the register for the blind and partially sighted. Ophthalmologists make the decision about eligibility, but it is the parent's decision to register. There are several advantages to this in services and benefits. The RNIB has details of what these are and how to go about registration.

What you need to know

- What is the nature of the child's visual impairment?
- What are the expected outcomes for this child? Will his eyesight change in any way over time?
- How much does he currently see, in which ways and under which conditions?
- How has the child responded/adapted to his specific visual difficulties and the use of his residual vision?
- What compensatory skills will the child need to develop?
- What are the implications for movement around the class and school?
- What implication does the above have for learning:

  - in the presentation of table-top activities?
  - in the lighting required?
  - in the size of lettering required?
  - in participating in physical activities?
  - in creative play – painting, modelling, etc?
  - in imaginative play – home-corner, miniature people?
  - using construction toys?
  - using computers?
  - at carpet time?
  - for stories and reading?

- What can be done to help the child integrate learning so that experiences become part of a whole rather than fragmented?
- Are there any specific difficulties that need to be addressed in unstructured times, either in the class or outside?
- How much experience does the child have in playing with other children? What do other children need to know and do in order to facilitate the child's participation?
- Does the child wear glasses? Are there implications for the use and care of these?
- What arrangements need to be in place for mobility training?

General learning needs

Several of the other difficulties described in this chapter will also apply to the child who has an overall learning difficulty, in particular those to do with communication and behaviour. A child who has a developmental delay in cognitive skills is also likely to behave like a much younger child. The greatest difficulty for those working in an early years setting is that young children are often strongly self directed and within an educational establishment they are often required to follow directions. Some do this quite happily, but others are more resistant. Finding an appropriate balance that allows for freedom of choice but extends learning challenges the skills of early years teachers.

Those children who have had, or who are having, an emotionally distressing time may also find it difficult to concentrate, learn, remember, problem solve or play happily with other children.

What you need to know

- What are the child's learning styles? Which are being used most?

  - Watching and copying?
  - Physical – needs to engage the whole body much of the time?
  - Experimental – seeing what happens?
  - Creative/problem-solving – making up stories, symbolic play?
  - Listening, asking questions?

- What is helpful in maintaining concentration?

  - Type of activity – which?
  - Doing things with adults/children?
  - Time of day?

- Is there anything that is particularly distracting for the child?
- What does the child enjoy doing? What interest could link in with activities, e.g. animals, a new baby, football? What else stimulates the child's motivation?
- In which circumstances does the child appear to learn best?

Following directions: what you need to know

What supports the child in following directions?

- Gaining visual attention – ensuring they are looking at the speaker?
- Using their name?
- Standing close to them?
- Making directions short and simple (but grammatically correct)?
- Checking understanding?
- Praising people next to them for following instructions?
- Praising them for part-compliance?
- Starting something with them?
- Reminding and reinforcing?
- Review and reinforcement (telling them what they have done well)?

Being independent: what you need to know

- Will the child do things independently or needs encouragement to try?
- Are new activities resisted? What helps in introducing different things?
- Does the child repeat known activities over and over again?
- Does the child need to know that it is acceptable to make mistakes?
- Does the child need 'larger than life' praise?
- What have parents found most useful in helping their child to learn?
- What are the learning priorities for the child?
- What are they presently able to do and what needs to happen next?

Emotional, social and behavioural needs

Structured situations are not suited to all small children. Sometimes a child is said to have a behavioural difficulty where, in fact, expectations are inappropriate for their age or developmental stage. Many small children require a high level of physical activity, a variety of activities, opportunities to stand and watch without doing anything active at all and plenty of time to play, develop imaginative skills and problem-solve in make-believe situations.

Other children demand a lot of adult attention, which is not easy or appropriate to provide. Sometimes these children have learned that they can gain attention by behaving in ways it is difficult to ignore. They need to gain attention by positive behaviours.

Some behaviours cluster together and may indicate that the child may be on the autistic spectrum. These behaviours include difficulties with:

- social interaction
- communication
- imagination.

These are usually associated with rigid, repetitive patterns of behaviour and often a fear of unfamiliar situations.

Children who are very unhappy are particularly worrying for teachers or early years practitioners, either because they express anger indiscriminately and other children get hurt, or because they withdraw from interaction. Some of these children may have experienced abuse, rejection or loss that affects their views of themselves and other people. Other children have simply not learned the skills they need to cooperate positively with other people, and these have to be taught.

Finding out

The most important things are:

- not to jump to conclusions about why a child is behaving in a way that is difficult to manage;
- to work closely with the parent to identify the difficulties and how they can best be addressed.

The health visitor, EP or any specialist teacher who has been working with the family at home will be helpful people to talk to.

What you need to know

- Does the child have any other difficulties, e.g. with learning or communication?
- What are the exact behaviours that are difficult? How frequently do they occur? What are the triggers for these, if any? Is there any pattern to them?
- What do parents say about how the child behaves at home?
- Which positive activities does he enjoy doing?
- What is known to be effective in encouraging willing cooperation?
- What soothes the child and has a calming effect?
- What does the child say about the way he feels?
- What are priorities for the child to learn:
  - about himself and others?
  - to manage the expression of his feelings?
  - to establish good interactions with other children?
  - to follow adult directions?
  - to settle to an activity?

Medical needs

Children may have a medical need in conjunction with a physical disability or other special need. The majority, however, will have a single condition such as epilepsy, asthma or allergy. As such, this will not be defined as SEN but as an additional educational need (AEN), but does require staff awareness. In most circumstances the school nurse or health visitor will be able to provide information and advice.

What you need to know

- The condition that the child has – are there any educational implications?
- What should be avoided wherever possible?
- What preventative measures/adaptations are helpful?
- What are the signs of any impending attack?
- What should be the immediate response of staff? What should happen next?
- Who should be contacted in the event of an attack at school?
- Does the child need medication to be administered at school? Where will this be kept and who will administer this?
- How will records be kept?
- Are there training implications? How can these be arranged?

Outcome of meetings

Staff and others may feel at the end of the initial planning meeting that there is an enormous amount to do. When a range of issues are thought through at the beginning, however, it saves much time and anxiety later on. Many of the plans and adaptations that make a great difference to a child and her family may in fact be quite small, and once they are in place they become routine. It is also useful to discuss at the outset how existing resources can be utilised most effectively and, without being negative, give everyone a sense of what is realistic. It is very helpful to know who is going to be doing what and how everything will be monitored. If something is not quite working as it should, then there are plans to review and adapt accordingly. It is worth remembering that it is not only *what* happens that matters, but also *how* it happens.

The following checklist can be used to help with initial general planning and also with the individual education plan that sets short-term targets for the child.

- Are any physical adaptations needed? What exactly are these?
- What curricular adaptations need to be made?
- Do any adaptations need to be made to the usual routine? What are these?
- Is any additional equipment needed? What will it be used for and who will monitor its use? Where will it be kept when not in use?
- What specific support is needed from:

  - the practitioners in the setting?
  - additional staff?
  - other children?
  - parents?
  - additional resources from the local authority?
  - others?

- What training needs have been identified? Who are appropriate trainers and who will make contact with them?
- Who will be responsible for monitoring learning and devising any IEP?
- What continuing communications will be put in place? Who will communicate with whom, when, how often and how? In particular, who will be taking responsibility for ongoing communication between home and the setting? What are the joint expectations for this?
- When is the date of the next meeting between home and the setting?
- When is the date of the next multi-disciplinary, family service plan and TAC meeting to review progress and needs?

Summary

The joint planning meeting should aim to reassure parents and practitioners alike that there is a co-ordinated team approach to meeting the child's needs. Everyone should have a good understanding of their own responsibilities and the support that is there to advise and help when necessary. Unless the child is placed in a special Children's Centre, however, many of the professionals in the team will be visitors rather than working on-site. It is how the whole school or nursery community also work together in responding to the child's needs that will make a difference to her happiness and progress in school.

Whether a program is called an Action Plan, an Individual Education Plan (IEP) or Personal Learning Plan, the following aspects are critical in maximising effective outcomes. We will use the original term IEP. This should be written for children who are not making progress through conventional, differentiated classroom teaching. The IEP needs to include:

- the learning intention(s);
- the learning strategy;
- the teaching strategy;
- the resources needed;
- the monitoring arrangements;
- the success criteria;
- the review arrangements.

The child and parents should be fully involved in deciding on the targets to be included. The professional judgement of the teacher or early years practitioner who writes the IEP is, however, essential as they have a thorough knowledge of:

- the child's learning style;
- the child's rate of learning;
- the child's current skill level;
- the curriculum requirements.

The review of an IEP should be a continuous process carried out with the child by their individual teacher or early years practitioner – but also evaluated at least twice each year by the SENCO, relevant teachers, the parents and the child.

What makes a quality IEP?

Children learn most when they are motivated, having fun and feeling confident. A good IEP will have a simple learning intention but a creative/fun teaching strategy.
It is important to state a learning intention so it is clear when that has been achieved. If a target is not achieved then the IEP needs to be analysed to consider what went wrong.

- Was the target too big a step?
- Did the child have all the entry skills required?
- Was the child motivated to practise the skill?
- Was the teaching strategy appropriate?
- Were the resources used appropriate (e.g. using a paintbrush and A3 paper instead of a pen and lined paper)?

The size of the target and the length of time that an IEP will run will depend upon the level of difficulty the child is experiencing. A child with significant additional needs will require IEPs with very small target step sizes that are reviewed regularly. Staff, parents and children will be motivated by the successful completion of targets.
This is adapted from information provided by Jenny Barclay and SENCO colleagues in Cornwall. Their website also includes a proforma for writing an IEP.

Figure 5.2 Good practice IEP planning in Cornwall.

Personal Communication Passports

This idea was first developed by Sally Millar (1995) to facilitate the inclusion and understanding of disabled people with sensory impairments who did not communicate through conventional language or speech. The passport was a written collection of key statements about the person relating to their basic daily lives that enhanced the quality of support and assistance they received. Ann Butt and Clare Cosser (2004) adapted the idea to support the transition of young children with learning difficulties into their mainstream settings or reception classes.

A PCP is a notebook or small photo album that consists of photographs and short statements written in the first person, so emphasising the child's voice. Parents and a key support person would compile the passport in partnership, and often include sections on:

- important things about me;
- my family and friends;
- things that make me happy and how I show this;
- what I need to help me understand what you want me to do.

(Adapted from Behaviour2learn, 2012)

The following is an extract from a passport used to support a child's transition into his reception class:

- I use signs, PECS, pointing or may take you to things to let you know what I want.
- If I am making 'Uh-Uh' sounds I am talking to you. Please take notice of me.
- Try asking me to do things first because I do understand a lot.
- I really like playing with cars or someone singing to me.
- I sometimes wander about, try giving me something to do.
- If I lift up my shirt it often means that I need changing.
- I need my food cut into tiny pieces.

(Examples courtesy of West Sussex Portage Service)

Figure 5.3 Personal Communication Passports (PCPs).

Chapter 6

In-school communication

Ethos, communication and effective schools

In this chapter we use the experience of good practice in primary schools to reflect on how to develop a supportive environment for children identified with SEN. Although the discussion focuses primarily on the school environment, many of the issues, principles and ideas can be generalised to other early years settings.

There is increasing acknowledgement that the culture of any organisation is closely linked to its effectiveness. Collaboration and communication are part of the overall ethos and the whole atmosphere of a school or early years setting is affected by the extent to which there is collegiality. The schools that are most effective have a culture in which the head has a clear vision of aims, but where everyone takes responsibility for meeting organisational goals. Where these goals include promoting high expectations for *all* children, there will be an incentive to clarify pupil needs, to work together both within the school and with others to raise the achievement of all. Clear lines of communication ensure that this works in practice, information is shared in a regular and accessible way, people know what their responsibilities are and where their support lies. Where individual needs are seen as a priority, time and resources are more likely to be available for planning and review. Where the ethos focuses on possibilities rather than problems, there will be a more relaxed and positive view of SEN. Where everyone in mainstream provision takes responsibility for meeting diverse needs, no-one has to face challenges alone.

Talking with others about a child

Communication about children in the staff room is powerful in establishing attitudes and expectations. Although discussing individuals and their families with other staff members can be very supportive and people do need an opportunity to express anxiety or exasperation, negative conversations, focusing exclusively on what the child cannot do or how badly behaved she is, undermines confidence and promotes self-fulfilling labels. Where a positive ethos pervades the culture of an establishment, this includes the way people talk about, as well as to, children and their parents. This includes the front-line administrative staff who are often the first people to meet with parents or talk with them on the telephone. First impressions of a school or nursery are powerful and school secretaries carry a special responsibility for the messages they convey.

The special needs co-ordinator

The legislation and guidance states that a member of staff in all mainstream schools and early education settings must be appointed to act as the special needs co-ordinator (SENCO). This person has a pivotal role in ensuring that relevant information about children is collated, appropriate learning targets are in place and there is effective communication both outside and inside school. The responsibilities inherent in this are central to the progress that children make. Although there has been a wide range of practice in different settings, the role and status of the SENCO is being gradually clarified and upgraded. There is increasing acknowledgement of the demands of the role and that careful thought is given to time allocation. It is appropriate that the SENCO is a member of the senior management team. The knowledge and skills that are now being developed in schools in relation to special needs are largely due to those individuals who have taken on the role of SENCO with such commitment.

Clarifying roles and responsibilities

In many schools and nurseries, the SENCO is the first point of contact for professionals and the second point of contact for parents, after the class teacher. There needs to be clarity about the distinct roles of the class teacher, head teacher and the SENCO about responsibility for SEN, in order to avoid confusion, duplication and bad feeling. Collaboration as a result of policy and planning is good practice – poor communication about who should be doing what is not. It is helpful to work out in advance who meets with parents when, how outcomes of meetings are communicated to others and the procedures for referrals. Arrangements for providing cover for professionals to meet with key staff can be problematic, and where responsibilities for this are agreed beforehand it ensures that professional time is put to best use.

Although the SENCO has primary responsibility for SEN matters, there are often issues that appropriately involve the head teacher. Heads and SENCOs need to agree who chairs and records major meetings such as those described in Chapter 5, how SEN records will be maintained and accessed, who attends case conferences outside school and how training will be co-ordinated. It is essential that the SENCO and head teacher meet together regularly to clarify the above, share information and monitor SEN practice in the school.

The SENCO and communication

The communication role of the SENCO is crucial in ensuring that there is good collaboration between school, parents and others. Information needs to be disseminated in a meaningful way to all those who are involved with a child. SENCOs need consultative skills as well as special needs knowledge; this involves being able to ask good questions, actively listen to both words and feelings and respond appropriately, define problems and strategies with others.

The communication role of the SENCO will be facilitated by:

• maintaining up-to-date contact information about carers and all professionals involved with a child – their names, addresses and telephone numbers – a proforma for this information is at Appendix 2;

- discussing reports from professionals with relevant staff in terms of their implications for the child's learning;
- arranging annual reviews of EHC Plans well in advance and having them in a block of time to facilitate the involvement of a range of agencies;
- having an effective filing system so that information is quickly accessible and can be updated easily – there are now good computer packages available for this;
- making relevant information about the child in the educational setting available to professionals and others (communication is often one-way rather than bi-directional, which underestimates the vital ongoing assessment role of key staff);
- facilitating meetings between professionals and key members of staff – possibly covering classes where necessary;
- facilitating home–school partnership between parents and key staff;
- being available at a regular time for informal discussions with staff;
- taking responsibility for ensuring there is effective liaison with support staff and temporary staff;
- maintaining and developing a resource base, including:

  - examples of good practice
  - training given with dates
  - in-school sources of expertise
  - information about external agencies, voluntary bodies and support groups
  - contact details of any keyworker or children's guardian;

- ensuring that transitions go smoothly by facilitating the exchange of information.

The role of the head teacher and governors is crucial in providing financial and other support to the SENCO, in enabling her to carry out her functions effectively. At a minimum level, this includes easy access to a telephone, desk and storage facilities. Time factors are also an issue that needs clarification with governors as well as the head.

The keyworker

There may be a designated keyworker for a child and family who works independently across health, education and care. It is sometimes useful, however, for the member of staff who has most contact with the child within the setting – or perhaps has a particularly special relationship with the child and/or parents – to be the child's keyworker on a day-to-day basis. This may be particularly valuable for those children whose needs are not deemed severe enough to warrant a full assessment for an EHC Plan. The keyworker might be an early years teacher but could also be any other appropriate adult working in the setting. If this happens, the roles of keyworker, SENCO and any other relevant staff must be clarified at the outset, together with decisions about how and when communication takes place.

Clarity, continuity and consistency

Communication with support staff

There are different kinds of support staff who may be involved with a child with SEN. They may be receiving some additional help from someone in school, or if the child is the subject of an EHC plan, then the local authority may be funding additional support, either directly or through the parent's budget. This may be support by a teacher or by a non-teaching assistant and could be someone coming in from an outside service. In some local authorities, support service teachers may liaise with the school in determining the role of the special needs assistant and to monitor this support rather than be directly involved themselves.

The relationship between a teacher and a support assistant can be complex. The following questions may be helpful in clarifying roles and responsibilities:

- How often will the support assistant be in the classroom or early years setting?
- How will exact days and times be negotiated?
- What is the support assistant there to do?
- How does this fit in with the child's learning targets, IEP or EHC Plan?
- What is the role of the class teacher in this plan?
- Who decides the day-to-day role of the support assistant?
- What should be the balance between individual work and group work?
- How will the child's inclusion into the class be supported by the assistant?
- Will the support assistant be spending time out of the classroom or nursery? How often, and what is the explicit purpose for this?
- What happens when the assistant is not there at the agreed times, e.g. on sick leave or on a course?
- What liaison time needs to be made available for the teacher and the support assistant to meet together? When will this be?
- How often should regular meetings with parents, the SENCO, the teacher and the support assistant take place? Who will arrange this?

Communication with lunchtime supervisors

Many children flourish within a structured setting, where there is good information about their needs and how best to meet these. It is in the unstructured times of the day when difficulties often arise, particularly at lunchtime. When children have had an unhappy experience during the dinner break, they may bring negative emotions back into the classroom in the afternoon. This does not help anybody. The adults supervising activities in the dining hall or the playground may not be aware of children's specific needs, what it is appropriate to expect from them, helpful approaches to adopt and how they can facilitate social interaction. Both information and skills are needed.

Possible approaches include:

- following agreement with parents, children's individual needs could be discussed with lunchtime supervisors;

- the link between behaviour and SEN should be made explicit, together with appropriate responses;
- additional training should be provided where necessary.

Tight budgets and contract specifications might militate against this good practice, but there are ways around this. Here are some of them:

- Senior staff provide occasional lunchtime supervision to enable supervisors to have training at this time.
- When there is a training day for staff, the lunchtime supervisors routinely have their own training programme; other arrangements are made for staff lunch; money may be available for providing whole- or half-day training from government funding programmes or other special arrangements.

JAMES (EHC Plan) has hearing impairment and learning difficulty – keep him in the front at carpet time, make sure he is looking directly at you. His left ear has better residual hearing. Has one-to-one support for two hours every morning.

CARLO has support from the behaviour support team on Tuesdays and Fridays. He responds best to a calm, but firm approach. If he throws a tantrum, the other children know to leave him to get over it – if he goes on for longer than ten minutes ask a member of staff to take him to the office. A raised voice makes him much worse.

DELLA (EHC Assessment Initiated) has physiotherapy exercises at lunchtime, just needs reminding to go to the medical room before she has her dinner.

SAMI: new arrival, speaks very little English and is very passive (learning difficulties?). The class are taking it in turns to play with her. They will be able to tell you whose turn it is this week.

Figure 6.1 SEN information for supply teachers.

- There is a keyworker lunchtime supervisor for individual children who links with the keyworker teacher or SENCO and then passes on information to colleagues on the child's needs and how to respond to these.
- Each class or nursery group links with one supervisor so that he or she gets to know the children and the teacher – the children are formally handed over by the teacher to the supervisor at lunchtime: this both enhances status for the supervisor and enables the two members of staff to work more closely together.
- Training happens 'on-site' during the lunch breaks, with trainers modelling inclusive activities with staff.

Communication with supply/casual teachers

Some best practice may be put at risk by a temporary teacher not being aware of a child's specific needs. Supply teachers may arrive at a moment's notice with little time to give them information. It is useful, therefore, to plan for this contingency in advance. The SENCO and the class teacher can take responsibility together for planning, with the SENCO ensuring that the information is with the supply teacher as soon as possible: it's not much use if it stays in the desk drawer. Where to find this information could be part of a whole school or early years pack for casual staff.

The information must be brief and to the point – no teacher coming into a class will have time to read a file! It may be useful to have just one piece of laminated card with four or five points on it, as in Figure 6.1.

Continuity

The best-laid plans within a school or early years provision can be thrown into disarray by a change in personnel. Sometimes there is no chance to prepare for this. If the communication in the school or nursery is good and several people have knowledge of and positive relationships with the children with SEN, then this will minimise any negative effects. The SENCO, however, should take responsibility for:

- communication with the member of staff who is 'taking over', however temporarily;
- arranging a meeting between this person and any support staff as soon as possible;
- communicating with the parents about any interim arrangements;
- communicating with the children about the situation in order to reduce any anxiety;
- reinforcing peer group support.

Keeping in touch

Sometimes children with SEN have many treatments or illnesses that mean they either are often absent from school or have intermittent long periods of absence. Keeping in touch with such children and their parents maintains good relationships and continuity. A weekly phone call is usually welcome, and arrangements for children to make contact are also valuable. This could be in the form of cards or pictures, as well as visits. Giving parents some ideas about curriculum-based activities helps to keep the child linked in with what is going on at school.

Child protection

It is sadly the case that children with disabilities and SEN are particularly vulnerable to abuse. All those working with such children need to be aware of this and maintain appropriate vigilance. Should emotional, physical or sexual abuse, or serious or persistent neglect, be suspected, careful monitoring needs to take place. Collated evidence should record incidents with dates, verbatim comments giving rise to concern and anything else that is worrying. This will be very helpful in the event that Common Assessment Framework procedures are initiated. Each school should have a designated teacher responsible for child protection, and each local authority will have published procedural guidelines. Teachers who think they have cause to be concerned need to have a three-way meeting with the designated teacher and SENCO to decide on a course of action. This discussion should determine whether a referral to the Local Safeguarding Board will be made at this point. Some Social Services departments have regular drop-in sessions for teachers and others working with children, which provide advice and guidance. It is important to maintain positive relationships with parents as much as possible, but it should always be made clear that teachers are obliged to follow up concerns and report any disclosures. As this may potentially cause conflict, any referral should be seen to be made by the school, not by any individual.

Communication with other children and other parents

Communication with other children

Young children do not have the same stereotypes and expectations as older children and adults. They are often able to give children with SEN an experience of acceptance that may put others to shame. They will, however, ask questions and be interested in why their classmate is different. There are a number of ways to address these issues. It is valuable to discuss what you might do with parents very early on. Some parents would be very reluctant to draw attention to their child's difficulties and differences. Others are happy for these to be discussed openly. Children have a right to be asked what they would like to happen and how much they want to be part of this.

Ideas for communicating SEN issues with children

Teachers can introduce activities in circle sessions about similarities and differences (Roffey, 2006, 2014). 'Pair shares' are good for this, where children find out two things that are the same about them and one that is different. This can begin with bodily features, e.g. some have fair hair while some have dark hair, then go on to less visible aspects such as strengths and personality traits. It is then a small step to look at differences where children need something extra, e.g. some children do not see as well as others and need glasses. With parents' agreement, teachers may then choose to introduce the needs of individual children without them feeling singled out.

There are now many books available that introduce more difficult topics to young children in story form. Reading and discussing these will help to raise issues and answer questions.

Adults with a range of disabilities (but who also have skills in interacting with young children) could be asked to come and talk with children who can then be encouraged to ask questions. Voluntary agencies may be able to put schools and nurseries in touch with people.

Some organisations can provide videos or even live drama groups to raise issues. When given by experienced and sensitive trainers, an experiential session can have a very positive impact on attitudes and understanding. This entails replicating some of the experiences that a child with difficulties (usually sensory) may have and what they need to do in their daily lives to adapt to these. This is also very useful for adults!

Sometimes children themselves may choose to tell their story to others and enjoy being the centre of attention. Again, any such proposal should not go ahead without parental agreement.

Communication with other parents

Communication on SEN issues needs to be part of the information that is given out to all parents when children begin school or nursery. An allusion to the school's philosophy on SEN may be useful even earlier, when parents first register their child or even when they make initial enquiries. Written information needs to:

*   state the school's SEN policy in understandable language;
*   outline the commitment to inclusive and anti-discriminatory practices and what this may mean;
*   clarify how the curriculum on offer will promote the skills of all;
*   state the school's policy on behaviour, including how positive, pro-social behaviour is being promoted and what happens when children's behaviour is challenging;
*   indicate lines of communication open to parents when they have a concern.

Conflict between parents can, at times, flare up in the playground, often over children's behaviour. Schools may be reluctant to address this directly with individuals, but do need to communicate the appropriate channels for raising issues of concern.

Transitions

Changes often come about because children grow older and move on. These transition periods are potentially difficult, and communication between people at these times makes a great deal of difference to the level of continuity and the smoothness with which transitions occur. People need to be aware that a settling-in period is necessary for both the teacher and the child as they get used to each other.

Between classes

This is usually not so dramatic a change as that between schools. The buildings and staff are familiar and, equally importantly, so are the other children. The overriding need is for good communication with the person who is taking on the major responsibility for the child, usually the class teacher. Ideally, a four-way meeting between the parent, the outgoing teacher, the incoming teacher and the SENCO will provide the following:

- basic information about the child and her SEN;
- awareness of any specific vulnerability;
- awareness of strengths and any special interests;
- information about others involved;
- appropriate approaches, adaptations and any specialist equipment;
- recent programmes and reviews;
- the progress the child has made on past and current targets;
- priorities for targets in the immediate future;
- arrangements for liaison with parents;
- any other essential information, such as other carers, language issues, etc.

If a support teacher or special needs assistant has been involved, they should also attend this in-school meeting. A few 'visits' to the teacher, perhaps with a friend, before the new term starts may also help with this process.

Between schools

Transition between pre-school provision and infant school or infants and juniors can be a time of anxiety for teachers, parents and children. Again, it is a question of reassurance and putting the right communications in place at the outset.

The EYFS Profile report, which takes place when children are five, gives Year 1 teachers information about each child's stage of development and learning needs, helping them to plan activities for children starting Key Stage 1. The Profile refers to the need to make reasonable adjustments for children with SEN and for the setting to develop relationships with other relevant professionals and the child's parent/carer so a clear picture is gained of the child's learning and development when they begin school.

The following strategies have met with a level of success. The more of them it is possible to put in place the better:

- The SENCO of the new provision attends a review of where the child is presently placed in order to gain as much information as possible and to meet with parents, any keyworker or significant professional.
- The SENCO opens a file that gives all contact details, progress towards learning goals and other relevant information, the EHC Plan if applicable, and examples of the child's work over time.
- The SENCO shares this information with the child's new teacher(s).
- The new class teacher visits the child in their nursery or infant setting for a morning or afternoon, discusses his progress with staff and ways in which they have dealt with any difficulties.
- The child is given an opportunity to visit his new school, perhaps accompanied by support staff.
- A planning meeting happens prior to intake, with parents and as many professionals as possible (see Chapter 5). This could be combined with the final review held in the old provision.

Case study: Hilda

Hilda, a child with Down syndrome, was due to transfer in September from her infant class to a junior school the other side of the borough. She had done well in her infant school and had been very settled there. Everyone was anxious about the move. The SENCO of the new school was able to attend her review in March and it was suggested that maybe a series of visits in the summer term would help with the transition. Her family thought this was an excellent idea. Hilda had a special needs assistant four mornings each week, so it was decided that she would accompany her to her new school for one morning each week for the second half of the summer term. Hilda really enjoyed this, and over the seven visits became familiar with the staff, found out how to get around the school and sat in on some lessons with the person who was to be her new teacher.

The teacher's worries about being able to meet Hilda's needs were addressed and she became more confident about the expectations that would be placed on her. The new teacher also met with Hilda's parents and established a rapport with them. When Hilda finally transferred in September she was one step ahead of the other children entering the school for the first time and was able to 'show them the ropes'. This raised her status and boosted her self-esteem.

The child who arrives mid-term

Sometimes a child arrives in a class with little or no information, and within a short while appears to be having difficulties. Chapter 4 suggests ways of approaching parents, but it may be that the child is in this situation because of disruptions in their home life. Many families in temporary accommodation are moved from one area to another before they finally settle. Some mothers may be escaping a violent situation and be very wary of giving out any information. Sensitivity to these issues is necessary but, where parents are agreeable, making contact with any previous educational provision or professionals is likely to be helpful. If it is the case that the child has been on waiting lists for services in other areas, then this might be communicated to current services so that she might receive some priority attention.

Children who leave to go to other schools

Likewise, when a child moves into another area, it is valuable if parental permission is sought to transfer information. Offering the SENCO of a new school or nursery an early telephone conversation might help the child to settle-in more quickly and allow appropriate provision to be made for him. An educational welfare officer might be involved if the child disappears without any information being given, especially if she is of school age.

Summary

The effectiveness of in-school communication makes a great deal of difference to children's happiness and progress in school. It is not only the SENCO and teachers who are critical in establishing a positive framework, but all those who are connected with the school and who come into contact with the child and her parents.

Case study: Starting primary school – top tips for families with children with SEN – City of York Council

In 2012 the City of York Council produced a booklet containing a range of information for parents/carers to support them in discussions as their child is preparing to start school. This complemented the 'Transition Toolkit' that was used by schools and early years settings in the authority to self-evaluate and develop their practice around transition for children from birth to six years old. The *Local Offer: Starting Primary School* booklet (City of York, 2012) includes 'Top Tips' on: choosing the right school; applying for a school place; and moving on from early years specialist services. There is a section on 'Frequently asked questions' which covers such topics as:

- My early support keyworker finishes when my child starts school, how can I continue to have a person who is my first point of contact?
- How do schools appoint a teaching assistant to work with my child?

- What are the arrangements for playtimes and lunchtimes so that the school can ensure my child's safety?
- Will my child be able to attend breakfast clubs and after-school clubs?

The emphasis throughout the booklet is on a working partnership between the receiving schools, parents, preschool and support services throughout transition. As well as the general pre-admission arrangements for all children, it is recommended that a 'family centred transition planning meeting' be held to support the individual child with SEN. A proforma for this meeting is included in the guide and parents are reassured that these discussions will often be set-up for them by a professional they know, such as their early support keyworker. Feedback from parents and practitioners who have experienced such meetings is included; for example:

> Informal, everyone had an equal say, parents views very welcome. Gave time to openly discuss the issues and concerns and provide reassurance.

> Very useful. It included a clear plan for transition and this was implemented well by all involved. Everyone involved knew what they needed to do and the family were clear as to what was going to happen from the action plan.
>
> (p. 16)

Guidance for holding these family-centred transition planning meetings is also included to support the development of consistent good practice. This includes:

- thinking carefully about the arrangements on the day, e.g. who by and how the family will be welcomed;
- specifying a timescale at the outset and ensuring enough time is allocated to each item that needs to be discussed;
- leaving sufficient time to record a clear plan of action;
- ensuring the family have a key person to contact.

The advice summarises that 'the key to a successful meeting is a relaxed atmosphere balanced with an appropriate level of structure so that everyone has an equal chance to contribute' (p. 29).

Parents are also advised that their early years setting or the receiving school may help them assemble a photograph book or video that they can share with their child as part of their preparations. They are also signposted to the fact that schools may run transition groups at their local Children's Centre which they are welcome to attend. The booklet also contains a copy of a 'Things I'd like you to know about me' record and suggests that parents can complete one of these about their child with the help of their pre-school. This information uses first-person statements to personalise the information, such as:

* Things I like/Things I don't like.
* Things I am good at/Things I need help with.
* I communicate by....
* I learn best when....

The guide can be provided in a number of community languages and is also available in accessible formats (e.g. large-print or CD-ROM).

Chapter 7

Issues affecting collaboration

I am the lynchpin – me and my husband – that co-ordinates all the services. I don't think there is one person who is thinking, because they think within their own little silo: in school they think of education; the paediatrician thinks about their medical health. I think, as a parent, you are the only one who thinks across the boundaries.
(Female participant, cited in Campbell-Hall *et al.*, 2009, p. 9)

This parent's perspective of the way services operate for her disabled child highlights the importance of collaborative working. Without collaboration the support provided becomes undermined by the stress created as families struggle to balance the input of well-meaning practitioners with their daily lives. Parents have reported: not knowing which service to approach to meet specific needs; being unclear which role each professional undertakes; receiving conflicting advice; and struggling to meet the demands of multiple appointments, assessments and programmes (Greco *et al.*, 2007). To help mitigate this, professionals need to commit to the development of integrated, collaborative practice both between and within services.

The first section of this chapter raises some of the structural and organisational issues involved in developing collaborative practices. The second addresses some of the interpersonal issues that impinge on the success of working relationships.

Structural and organisational issues

Working together: from the top down

Early years practitioners in their day-to-day work have always developed informal contacts and relationships with others outside the setting who are working with families. Health visitors, social workers, SLTs and Portage home visitors are commonly seen to be working alongside pre-school settings, particularly to support individual children with special needs. Such contacts were formalised by the agenda set by the *Every Child Matters* Green paper agenda (DfES, 2003) and the 2004 Children Act. Since then, services have been required to work together for the children and families they support, with a particular focus on identifying children at risk.

It takes time, however, to change traditional ways of working, and services may remain fragmented. Often, 'joined up thinking' has been against the odds and progress is often due to the determination of individuals rather than the organisational structures in which people work. The profile of the Every Child Matters agenda has become less prominent in early years policy and guidance emerging from central government, making local initiatives and creativity once again central to the development of collaborative working. Such tensions suggest that there are several factors influencing whether collaboration and co-ordination become routine and a reality nationwide:

- government policy, directives and incentives for developing integrated practice;
- effective liaison between government departments to ensure that the raft of changes they demand from public services interconnect and support clarity rather than confusion for people in their daily working lives;
- understanding by local politicians that joint funding for inter-agency work requires both vision and determination to change fragmented practices; is beneficial to children and their families; and is cost-effective in the long run;
- liaison between chief executives of local authorities and Health Service managers to develop frameworks for setting joint priorities and joint planning to meet objectives;
- commitment from senior managers to work together at the highest level – within local authorities this means that protection of individual budgets should be secondary to the development of inter-agency client-centred practices;
- professionals, and professional bodies, who focus on working together rather than defending their particular corner of expertise.
- the development of a culture in which inter-agency communication and understanding is given high priority and seen as an effective use of time;
- initial training and professional development that clarifies the contexts in which different people work and the perspectives that inform their actions;
- joint training and the development of services that provide a 'multi-disciplinary team' approach to meeting needs;
- the appointment of personnel whose job description includes a liaison role with other agencies and dissemination of relevant information.

Without the senior organisational and professional will and commitment implied in the above framework, the reality of effective collaboration may continue to depend on individuals who are determined to make it happen in their specific contexts. When these individuals leave, collaboration may cease. Conversely, too much pressure for change from the top down can be counter-productive and demand for quick results may take over from sustainable service development (Pemberton and Mason, 2008). In any drive towards integrated working it can be easy to lose sight of the core aim of collaboration: improved support for families. Interestingly, parents often suggest that low-key integration is a priority for them, delivered by agencies being located in a single centre and maintaining effective communication between practitioners from different disciplines. High-level complex integration of services, such as merging social service and education departments, is of less significance (Campbell-Hall et al., 2009).

Case study: The Bromley Early Support Full Programme Team

The Early Support team in Bromley consists of two co-ordinators, a parent representative and two administrators. To be referred, children and families have to have at least three health professionals and one other practitioner working with them, not including their paediatrician, health visitor or GP. Referrals go to the co-ordinators, who then carry out an initial home visit to get a picture of the agencies involved and start to work towards a more joint approach. The team may also be linked up with families and young children who are in hospital during post-natal care. By meeting the families before they return home, the Early Support team are able to take on an immediate key working role and relieve the pressure on parents to manage the multi-disciplinary input that becomes available. A prime area of work has been to develop a close working relationship with the local hospital consultants and special care baby units.

A family will have a keyworker who will visit their home regularly, acting as a contact point for providing information, and following up issues on behalf of the parents. The keyworker is chosen by the family from the range of professionals they see with their child, such as a Portage home visitor or a member of staff at their local pre-school. If the child and family have been linked up with the service very early on in hospital then it is likely that the team co-ordinator will initially take on the key working role.

As the key working team can be very diverse, and being a keyworker is often an additional part of a professional's primary role, co-ordination of the group is essential. This is achieved through half-termly meetings in which the keyworkers liaise with the Early Support co-ordinators. These meetings allow those involved to share information and updates from their various service perspectives. The keyworkers can also discuss aspects of their support for individual families, so developing their practice on the basis of any feedback they receive. Keyworkers are required to submit periodic summaries to the co-ordinator outlining their input and the current situation with their focus family. It is the responsibility of the Early Support team to ensure that the keyworkers have up-to-date information that can be passed on to families, which include details of local and national services as well as benefits and legal advice.

The other main service that the Early Support team provides is facilitating a multi-agency meeting. The team sets up a meeting whenever the family feels it could be helpful and only with the professionals that the family want to attend. In practice the discussions are generally held every few months. The focus of the multi-agency meeting is to agree a Family Service Plan that records the arrangements for supporting the parents and their child in the ensuing months. The team in Bromley has found a high level of commitment by professionals to the meetings, despite increasing demands on resources and time. They feel this is because the collaborative approach is recognised as being of value by both parents and practitioners.

Since 2011 Bromley has been one of the pathfinder local authorities testing the feasibility of key reforms envisaged within the English government's Green Paper 'Support and Aspiration: A new approach to special educational needs and disability' (DfE, 2011a). This means that in the future, the Family Service Plans for those children who meet the threshold criteria will be incorporated into the statutory EHC Plans. In addition, Bromley are researching how disabled children and their families may be offered keyworker support beyond the child's early years, potentially until they are 25.

Keyworker role and responsibilities

A keyworker offers support with the following:

- identifying and addressing the needs of the child and being a source of emotional and practical support;
- offering a single point of contact for the family and the professionals working with their child. A keyworker can signpost the family to other services available to support their child, making referrals where appropriate;
- ensuring parents and carers have access to the full range of Early Support materials as appropriate;
- supporting families when using the Family Pack and Family File;
- helping families look forward to their child's next stage of development, and to effect a smooth transition to school;
- offering ongoing support for families at the multi-agency meetings;
- ensuring the Family Service Plan continues to meet the child's needs and that action points are carried out;
- ensuring other professionals are kept aware of factual information, e.g. change of medical needs, change of address, professionals leaving or joining a child's team.

The role is achieved by the following:

- proactive regular contact between the keyworker and the family, face to face or by phone;
- a family-centred approach;
- regular supervision of keyworkers from the Early Support team, including support meetings for keyworkers;

- an agreed system with keyworkers for record keeping with the Early Support team;
- provision of induction training and ongoing training for keyworkers;
- individual support and advice to keyworkers from the Early Support team.

(Adapted from Bromley Early Support Programme Leaflet, 2012)

Resources

> The question of resources is the acid test of the commitment for joint action.
>
> (NLIAH, 2007)

Collaborative working requires staffing and systems to support it. Roles may change, equipment may be necessary and administrative support will be essential. In a small pre-school setting the SENCO may be required to attend more planning meetings for families as part of a multi-agency team. 'Cover' for their absence will have to be provided, which inevitably incurs costs. At whatever level, a partnership approach to resource responsibilities needs to be taken. Tensions between services will be eased if the resourcing of collaborative work is seen as equally shared. The financial position of the voluntary or community sector needs to be respected and public agencies may be expected to take on a higher proportion of costs. This may in itself bring inequalities in terms of power and influence within working relationships and needs to be acknowledged and addressed.

There are no simple answers, but it may be useful to consider the following:

- The more transparency there is about resources, the more accountable people will be for how they are spent. This applies to local authorities and to individual schools, Children's Centres and other pre-school settings.
- Central joint planning is likely to make better use of existing resources.
- The more creative and flexible policy makers and budget holders are, the better use they will be able to make of existing resources.
- Where joint planning takes a longer-term view, less resources will be required to fund expensive crisis intervention.
- The more joint structures there are, the less need there will be for expensive one-off decision-making meetings.
- The less duplication there is, the less waste of resources there will be.

The resourcing of collaborative practices is justified by the recognition that joint working has a close relationship with overall service effectiveness. For example:

- The more emphasis there is on collaborative early intervention, the better the outcomes for individual children.
- When resources are allocated to developing partnership with parents, there will be greater understanding about needs, expectations and interventions. This empowers parents to be more effective.

- Where the promotion of effective channels of communication is a priority both in and out of settings, the more effective each professional and each service will be.
- The more emphasis put on working together, the more supported individuals will feel.
- The more supported individuals feel, the more able they will be to meet children's needs.

Collaboration therefore encourages the more efficient use of scarce resources and its benefits can be perceived as outweighing any potential costs. It may take time to develop a co-ordinated and coherent service for all families, but:

> a truly integrated set of services can provide support for children and their families that goes beyond the sum of its parts, helping to develop a more holistic understanding of each child, and ultimately increasing the certainty that children will receive the support that they need.
>
> (Tickell, 2011, p. 26)

Time

The variable nature of settings and the range of people involved mean there is no guaranteed recipe for team success. However, 'an effective group of early years practitioners emerges as the result of an investment of time and energy of all concerned' (Read and Rees, 2010, p. 43).

Planning ahead …

Crisis management – today, tomorrow … and next week

Time issues bridge the organisational and interpersonal levels of working together. Developing relationships, getting to know and understand each other's working practices, clarifying joint objectives and ironing out misunderstandings takes time, at least initially. Planning the process and mechanisms to develop collaboration may be a lengthy phase in team building, particularly to ensure that everyone is viewed as an equal partner, including those viewed as service users. Making sure that parents do not feel they are being a 'nuisance' means taking the time to listen. Finding out about a child's needs properly from both the family and the young person themselves does not happen overnight. The day-to-day responsibilities of any role coupled with issues of variable staff resources can make prioritising time to develop joined-up working difficult. When personnel are in short supply but the demands of the job increase incrementally, time becomes the most precious resource of all. Services that experience staff cuts year on year but are expected to carry the same workload will inevitably be less effective. In such situations time priorities need to be renegotiated with senior managers and then communicated to service users.

Setting priorities

Time is finite. Demands are not. Priorities need to be made. When initial planning does not happen, time is spent re-inventing the wheel, repeating the same information to different people, having impromptu crisis intervention meetings and generally not putting valuable time to the best use. Meetings that are planned well in advance so that everyone can prepare for them are likely to be more effective. When information is kept where everyone knows how to get at it quickly, no one has to spend hours in futile searches. When support systems are set up so that everyone knows when other people are available, less time is taken up in chasing individuals. When inter-agency work is seen as productive, practitioners make their attendance at joint meetings a priority. This may save time and effort in trying to make contact with elusive colleagues.

For collaborative teams of any size the importance of establishing a regular programme of meetings that accommodates the routines of all those who need to attend should not be underestimated. Mary Read and Mary Rees, while exploring the practicalities of developing teams in early years settings, suggest that keeping a meeting log as a record of the programme helps reflection and adjustments to the schedule. This records not only the attendees and purpose of the meeting, but also who made the most contributions; what was achieved; and comments on the meeting's effectiveness by the participants (Read and Rees, 2010). The log can be used to assess the relative benefits of time invested and outcomes.

Maybe the real world is not as tidy as this – but there does need to be a commitment by senior managers to allow time for planning across all levels. A balance needs to be struck between providing clear expectations for their workforce and genuinely valuing collaborative dialogue with those practitioners who are in regular contact with the child and his family.

Leadership

Leaders need to inspire, nurture, support and communicate with individuals, teams and networks across and within different organisations. It is likely that traditional approaches to leadership will not be appropriate in collaborative situations and, importantly, there is a need to focus on processes and skills that do not always reside in formally appointed leaders (NLIAH, 2007; Armstrong, 2012). In many ways the leadership of an integrated team is less about being leader 'of' the group and more about leading 'with' the group alongside. The leader is less engaged in imposing a strategy or enforcing standards and needs to focus on encouraging innovation and compromise. This particular style of leadership is often called dispersed or distributive. Table 7.1 summarises the contrast between the collaborative and more traditional leader.

The challenge facing those in leadership positions who are trying to develop collaborative working is how to nurture participation in decision making and encourage collective problem solving. In an early years setting, parents and children also need to be central to this participatory approach, not just practitioners. Structures and systems need to be in place to formalise such collaborative practice, which stretch beyond good liaison with families regarding their child. A leader who is developing a collaborative approach in their setting creates mechanisms to involve parents and children in policy making and governance decisions.

Sharing information

An essential part of successful team working is organising effective communication so that information can be shared and there are clear lines of communication between people in different roles. To support collaborative practice within a setting, systems will be in place to ensure that people know what is happening and what has happened. This can range from face-to-face briefings to handover diaries or noticeboards. Some settings may prioritise whole-team meetings at the start of each day to ensure that everyone is aware of the possible challenges and opportunities of the sessions ahead. Others may have to consider organisational factors (e.g. work patterns) or physical circumstances (e.g. the availability of a meeting room) when planning to develop communication systems in their team. These may seem simple, orthodox

Table 7.1 Leadership styles

Traditional leadership	Collaborative leadership
Hierarchical	Non-hierarchical and inter-organisational
Evokes followership	Evokes collaboration and concerted action
Takes charge; seizes the reins of an organisation	Provides the necessary catalyst or spark for action
Takes responsibility for moving followers in certain directions	Takes responsibility for convening stakeholders and facilitates agreements for collective action
Heroic; provides the right answers	Facilitative; asks the right questions
Has a stake in a particular solution or strategy	Has a stake in getting to agreed-upon outcomes but encourages divergent ways to reach them

Source: NLIAH, 2007, p. 15.

practices, but they can be the foundations of working collaboratively and productively. This is because 'a team which is able to communicate openly and clearly, avoids wasting time on frustration and misunderstanding' (Read and Rees, 2010, p. 49).

Open communication and sharing of information between different settings or services also 'underpins good integrated working and is important for promoting good outcomes for children and families, as well as protecting them from significant harm' (DfE, 2011c, p. 70). As a result of the inquiries into the tragic deaths of two children, Victoria Climbie in 2003 and Baby Peter in 2009, the importance of transparency and efficiency in information sharing has become a priority at all levels within the childcare sector. The impact of issues of confidentiality on communication between agencies has been reduced through such measures as the introduction of Local Safeguarding Boards (cross-agency bodies that oversee child protection procedures in every local authority) and the Common Assessment Framework (a multi-agency approach to assessing the needs of vulnerable young children and their families). The importance of maintaining the balance between preserving the confidentiality of service users and sharing information to ensure the wellbeing of young children has become more widely appreciated. Consequently, more sophisticated advice has become available for practitioners. The list of 'seven golden rules for information sharing' published by the government in England in 2008 illustrates the intricacies of the issues and provides useful guidance for all practitioners:

1. *Remember that the Data Protection Act is not a barrier to sharing information* but provides a framework to ensure that personal information about living persons is shared appropriately.
2. *Be open and honest* with the person (and/or their family where appropriate) from the outset about why, what, how and with whom information will, or could be shared, and seek their agreement, unless it is unsafe or inappropriate to do so.
3. *Seek advice* if you are in any doubt, without disclosing the identity of the person where possible.
4. *Share with consent where appropriate* and, where possible, respect the wishes of those who do not consent to share confidential information. You may still share information without consent if, in your judgment, that lack of consent can be overridden in the public interest. You will need to base your judgment on the facts of the case.
5. *Consider safety and wellbeing:* Base your information sharing decisions on considerations of the safety and well-being of the person and others who may be affected by their actions.
6. *Necessary, proportionate, relevant, accurate, timely and secure:* Ensure that the information you share is necessary for the purpose for which you are sharing it, is shared only with those people who need to have it, is accurate and up-to-date, is shared in a timely fashion, and is shared securely.
7. *Keep a record* of your decision and the reasons for it – whether it is to share information or not. If you decide to share, then record what you have shared, with whom and for what purpose.

(HM Government, 2008, p. 11)

Case study: Karen

Karen, a behaviour support teacher, was asked to work with Peter, a young boy with hydrocephalus. Her assessment of the situation provided some interesting and useful insight:

> Peter was considered to be aggressive by the teaching staff, not only because of incidents in the playground but also because of assumptions regarding his condition. The only information that staff had received was via informal discussion with Peter's mother. She did not want her child 'labelled' and therefore had actively resisted any school contact with health professionals. Staff were under the impression that a child with hydrocephalus would inevitably be aggressive.

Following the concern that the school were expressing about incidents in the playground she finally agreed to go ahead with a multi-disciplinary meeting. The professionals who attended were able to dispel the perception that hydrocephalus and aggression were inextricably linked. Karen's assessment also pointed to other reasons for the rise in incidents in the playground.

This additional information gave staff a fresh perspective and understanding. Interventions were planned for group work on 'safe playground behaviour' and extending play opportunities. This improved the situation for everyone.

Joint training

One way of developing collaborative practice is multi-agency professional development. This could be:

- sessions taken together with outside speakers;
- sessions in which professionals describe their practices to others;
- joint delivery on specific topics.

Training could be given by: parents and professionals on their perspectives of an aspect of SEN; teachers and professionals presenting together; or any combination of different agencies. Workshops where participants have opportunities to discuss and problem solve with each other in mixed groups are more likely to foster mutual understanding than relying solely on presentations. Joint training promotes the breaking down of stereotypes and prompts services and individuals to work through barriers to collaborative working (Charles and Horwarth, 2009).

Interpersonal issues

Much of the good collaboration that presently takes place all over the country happens where mutually supportive relationships are flourishing. Even when structures to promote inter-agency work are in place, these will not thrive unless there is understanding, trust and value put upon the individual knowledge, skills and approaches of all the collaborative partners. Developing such relationships moves collaboration beyond the way that services are organised or tasks are shared between individuals. 'Working together' becomes being part of a learning community in which people are given time to learn from each other, reflect on challenges and opportunities together and jointly plan a way forward.

Building such a collaborative community is not, however, easy to achieve when faced with professional jealousies and protectionism. Value systems, philosophies, attitudes, expectations and even the language people use can all impact on any attempts to work collaboratively. Team members from different services can fall back on assumptions and stereotypes about other agencies. Tensions can also develop if practitioners in integrated teams feel they are unclear of their role and in many ways that they have lost control. As this professional observes, working in a multi-agency service can lead to marginalisation rather than new opportunities for partnership:

> Your identity starts to dissolve in other areas – the new culture that you find yourself in – and I think you can end up feeling an outsider in both actually.
>
> (Rose, 2009, p. 7)

Collaborative working therefore needs to address interpersonal issues as well as structural or organisational matters. This includes an effort to: balance power and authority; keep families and children at the centre of the service; and communicate effectively.

Balancing power

Partnerships are more likely to be successful when there is a balance of power and authority. If one partner is conscious that he has more status or another convinced that her views are right because she has more experience, then any attempt at partnership is immediately undermined.

- Collaboration is not talking to other people. It is doing things together.
- Sharing decisions is not checking out your decisions with someone else. It is making them together.
- Communication is listening as well as talking.
- Equality is everyone taking responsibility for both the problem-definition and the solutions.

This may be particularly difficult where there is a hierarchy or structural power base within the partnership. It is possible, however, to put seniority to one side in order to have a team approach for specific pieces of work. If anyone is to be a true collaborative partner, they must not be in a position where there is a conditional clause to their involvement. This is especially true for parents. For example, a family who are told 'if you do this then we will not exclude your child' are being allowed to collaborate purely on the terms of the (powerful) professionals. Professionals need to be aware that they can often unintentionally assume a dominant position in their relationship with families and children, as the following parent experienced during her son's assessment:

> The first educational psychologist that we had, again a nice enough girl, came out to the house a week before the pre-scat [Pre-School Community Assessment Team] and chatted and sort of met Alan for the first time and then came to the review meeting as the one with the most power, yet the least knowledge of Alan. She had just met him and basically came with a checklist to say Alan can do this, or can't do that, tick, tick, tick.
>
> (Mollard, 2003, p. 81)

Recognising your powerful position as a practitioner and being prepared to challenge it by doing things in less established ways is an important contribution that you can make to develop collaboration. You can also use your power to hand over decision making to those within the partnership who have not traditionally been given such responsibilities, especially on issues that impact them.

Keeping the families at the centre

> Each of the partners has their own agenda.... So I feel that I am always pulled a lot in different directions.
>
> (Moran *et al.*, 2007, p. 147)

This social worker's view of working in a multi-agency family support team highlights that the differences between practitioners can cause real pressure and tension within a team. It is inevitable that professionals will not always agree – even professionals within the same discipline can hold disparate views and work from different theoretical standpoints. People who work in the public and voluntary sector are often passionate about what they do and, although their level of commitment is laudable, they may become blinkered to the potential usefulness of other perspectives. Collaborative working requires practitioners to embrace these different perspectives and use them to develop more informed practice.

If teams struggle to work in this way, if the differences between the agencies that have been brought together to collaborate become barriers, then parents may find themselves lost in the debate. One answer is to empower parents to take more control over the decisions for their children. Differing views can be presented to parents with the advantages and disadvantages of each. If arguments for and against are made in a professional and non-emotive way, the parent can be left to assess what is on offer. Parents may be aided in their deliberations by voluntary organisations, parent supporters or advocates; it is helpful if they have opportunities to ask questions and, where appropriate, visit provision.

Beyond individual situations, collaboration with parents as a group is recognised as an essential component of integrated service development. This has been supported by government policy in England since 2009, when the 'Aiming High for Disabled Children' strategy was introduced. From this time it has been obligatory for local areas to not only consult with parents about local services but also to involve them at a strategic level to shape provision. Funding has been made available to localities to set up parent forums to co-ordinate and develop parent participation at this level. Significantly, evidence shows that such involvement enhances parents' confidence and contentment as a group and leads to the all-round improvement of services.

Keeping families at the centre at both individual and strategic level provides focus for all those working collaboratively. Making a commitment to family-centred practice helps cut through the interpersonal and inter-professional differences that can strain joined-up working. The principle that the wellbeing of the child is central can be the foundation for building mutual understanding, respect and tolerance. It can also help practitioners cope with the shifts in thinking that multi-disciplinary work often entails. As one professional facing such changes in ways of working noted: 'The vast majority of people are interested in the child's welfare and as soon as you tap into that they'll be happy with it' (Rose, 2009, p. 5).

Communicating effectively

A multi-agency team of practitioners in Scotland identified the following principles for developing effective communication in their team:

- We will share information.
- We will listen to what people have to say.
- We will respect confidentiality.
- We will ensure good systems of communication.
- We will involve, consult and actively build good relationships.

(GIRFEC in Lanarkshire, 2011)

As well as the formal strategies that have been discussed earlier in this chapter, these principles suggest that interpersonal factors can also have an impact on positive relationships and working together. People within teams also need to be able to respond to each other professionally and supportively, however good the systems. They need to feel confident that the information they share will be valued and that they can be honest with their colleagues. The setting needs to develop its listening culture not only with children and families, but among its staff. It needs to nurture a belief that everyone's voice will be heard by showing that it recognises the contribution that individuals make. It is recognised that 'honest and sincere positive feedback oils the wheels of the daily task and enables all team members to benefit from both giving and receiving affirmation' (Read and Rees, 2010, p. 48). 'Respect' may stay at the level of rhetoric unless specific interpersonal practices are put in place (Roffey, 2005).

The following promote mutual respect as part of everyone's reality in joint meetings:

- ensuring no single voice in a meeting dominates;
- giving everyone a chance to contribute to the agenda;
- giving non-verbal messages of equality – such as how people are addressed, and seating arrangements;

- facilitating the involvement of others by asking open questions and showing interest in what they have to say;
- resisting interruptions and other behaviour that can be interpreted as a put-down;
- acknowledging and building on people's ideas;
- speaking positively to and also about others – negativity in meetings is toxic to collaboration and positive outcomes;
- seeking solutions and staying with the positive rather than using up valuable time unpicking the reasons for problems;
- being empathic to the experiences of others without saying that you 'know how they feel' – you don't;
- being aware of time pressures and therefore beginning and ending meetings at the stated time.

Collaborative working can bring new strains on the area of communication as practitioners may find themselves taking on new roles and responsibilities, and having to communicate with unfamiliar colleagues. People may need to seek more advice from each other or be required to share information with someone who is in a different position of authority. There may also be an increased likelihood of differences of opinion. However, such differences do not need to be suppressed – as this practitioner working in a collaborative team reflects, they can be a source of creativity:

> If there wasn't any challenge, if there wasn't any discussion around it, if there wasn't a different viewpoint, how could you be sure that the decision that was made was the best possible one?
>
> (Rose, 2009, p. 9)

Summary

The policy framework since 2000 has indicated an emerging awareness that effective multi-agency cooperation is central to meeting the needs of vulnerable children and their families. But top-down policy initiatives can be fragile and subject to shifts in the political climate. For example, from 2010 the coalition government in England gave significantly less prominence to the 'Every Child Matters' agenda, which had been a cornerstone policy of the previous administration. Faced with such shifts, maintaining collaborative working at a practice level becomes increasingly important.

'Working together can be wonderful when everyone pulls together.' This quote from a professional working with early years children and their families sums up the rationale for collaboration, but also suggests that it is not always a straightforward process. This chapter has summarised some of the many complex issues that may be involved in 'pulling together' but, whatever the challenges, we must continue to strive for ever more collaborative practices. For when we are successful, families are empowered and supported, professionals feel more valued and have greater job satisfaction and, most importantly, children are more likely to have an optimum learning experience. One parent's reaction to experiencing collaborative working is a fitting conclusion:

The day that two people came from different places, arrived together and said they wanted to try out a joint assessment I wanted to shout 'Yipppeee!' But I just said 'OK, that's good'. But inside I thought this was a breakthrough. It was great to see them working together like that. I only had to answer one set of questions and it seemed so much more sensible.

(Mother, cited in Carter et al., 2005, p. 536)

Information and resources on special educational needs

General information and advice on SEN

Advisory Centre for Education (ACE)
 36 Nicholay Road, London N19 3EZ
 ☎ General advice line 0300 011 5142
 ☎ Office 0208 407 5142
 www.ace-ed.org.uk
 enquiries@ace-ed.org.uk

Children in Scotland
 Princes House, 5 Shandwick Place, Edinburgh EH2 4RG
 ☎ 0131 228 8484
 ☎ Fax 0131 228 8585
 www.childreninscotland.org.uk
 info@childreninscotland.org.uk

Council for Disabled Children
 8 Wakley Street, London EC1V 7QE
 ☎ 0207 843 1900
 ☎ Fax 0207 843 6313
 www.councilfordisabledchildren.org.uk
 cdc@ncb.org.uk

Invalid Children's Aid Nationwide (ICAN)
 8 Wakley Street, London EC1V 7QE
 ☎ 0845 225 4073
 www.ican.org.uk
 info@ican.org.uk

National Association for Special Educational Needs (NASEN)
 Nasen House, 4–5 Amber Business Village, Amber Close, Amington,
 Tamworth, Staffordshire B77 4RP
 ☎ 01827 311 500
 ☎ Fax 01827 313 005
 www.nasen.org.uk
 welcome@nasen.org.uk

Organisations which promote the inclusion of children with SEN in mainstream education

The Alliance for Inclusive Education
  336 Brixton Road, London SW9 7AA
  ☎ 0207 737 6030
  www.allfie.org.uk
  info@allfie.org.uk

Centre for Studies on Inclusive Education (CSIE)
  The Park Centre, Daventry Road, Knowle, Bristol BS4 1DQ
  ☎ 01173 533 150
  ☎ Fax 01173 533 151
  www.csie.org.uk
  admin@csie.org.uk

Early years organisations

British Association for Early Childhood Education
  136 Cavell Street, London E1 2JA
  ☎ 0207 539 5400
  ☎ Fax 0207 539 5409
  www.early-education.org.uk
  office@early-education.org.uk

Early Childhood Unit
  National Children's Bureau
  8 Wakley Street, London EC1V 7QE
  ☎ 0207 843 6000
  ☎ Fax 0207 278 9512
  www.ncb.org.uk/ecu

Legal advice

Coram Children's Legal Centre
  University of Essex, Wivenhoe Park, Colchester, Essex CO4 3SQ
  ☎ Advice Line 08088 020 008
  ☎ 01206 877 910
  ☎ Fax 01206 877 963
  www.childrenslegalcentre.com

National Youth Advocacy Service
  Egerton House, Tower Road, Birkenhead, Wirral CH41 1FN
  ☎ Helpline 0300 330 3131
  ☎ 0151 649 8700
  ☎ Fax 0151 649 8701
  www.nyas.net
  help@nyas.net, legal@nyas.net

Parents for Inclusion
   336 Brixton Road, London SW9 7AA
   ☎ Helpline: 0800 652 3145
   ☎ 0207 738 3888
   www.parentsforinclusion.org
   info@parentsforinclusion.org

British Association for Early Childhood Education
   136 Cavell Street, London E1 2JA
   ☎ 020 7539 5400
   www.early-education.org.uk
   office@early-education.org.uk

The Children's Society
   Edward Rudolf House, Margery Street, London WC1X 0JL
   ☎ 0207 841 4400
   www.childrenssociety.org.uk

Parent support

Contact a Family
   209–211 City Road, London EC1V 1JN
   ☎ Helpline: 0808 808 3555
   ☎ 0207 608 8700
   ☎ Fax 0207 608 8701
   www.cafamily.org.uk
   helpline@cafamily.org.uk
   Among other things provides support to parents and professionals who are
   setting up and running groups – see website at www.makingcontact.org

Independent Parental Special Educational Advice
   Hunters Court, Debden Road, Saffron Walden CB11 4AA
   ☎ Advice Line 0800 018 4016
   ☎ Tribunal Helpline 0845 602 9579
   ☎ 01799 582030
   www.ipsea.org.uk

National Parent Partnership Network
   8 Wakley Street, London EC1V 7QE
   www.parentpartnership.org.uk

Network 81
   10 Boleyn Way, West Clacton, Essex CO15 2NJ
   ☎ Helpline 0845 077 4055
   ☎ Fax 0845 077 4058
   www.network81.org
   network81@hotmail.co.uk

Voluntary organisations concerned with specific SEN

Allergy UK (British Allergy Foundation)
  Planwell House, LEFA Business Park, Edgington Way, Sidcup, Kent DA14 5BH
  ☎ Helpline 01322 619 898
  ☎ Fax 01322 611 655
  www.allergyuk.org
  info@allergyuk.org

Asthma UK
  Summit House, 70 Wilson Street, London EC2A 2DB
  ☎ 0800 121 6255
  www.asthma.org.uk
  info@asthma.org.uk

National Autistic Society
  393–395 City Road, London EC1V 1NG
  ☎ Helpline 0808 800 4104
  ☎ 020 7833 2299
  ☎ Fax 020 7833 9666
  www.autism.org.uk
  nas@nas.org.uk

Autism Cymru
  62 Newport Road, Cardiff CF24 0DF
  ☎ 02920 463 263
  ☎ 01970 625 256
  www.autism-cymru.org
  info@autismcymru.org

Royal National Institute of Blind People (RNIB)
  105 Judd Street, London WC1H 9NE
  ☎ Helpline 0303 123 9999
  www.rnib.org.uk
  helpline@rnib.org.uk
  Supporting early years education materials:
  www.rnib.org.uk/professionals/education/support/guidance/earlyyears/Pages/
  early-years.aspx

National Blind Children's Society
  Bradbury House, Market Street, Highbridge, Somerset TA9 3BW
  ☎ 0278 764 770
  www.nbcs.org.uk
  enquiries@nbcs.org.uk

Entrust Care (formerly Association for Brain Damaged Children & Young Adults)
  Clifton House, 3 St Paul's Road, Foleshill, Coventry CV6 5DE
  ☎ 02476 665 450
  www.entrustcare.co.uk

Brittle Bone Society
  Grant-Paterson House, 30 Guthrie Street, Dundee DD1 5BS
  ☎ 01382 204 446
  ☎ Fax 01382 206 771
  www.brittlebone.org
  contact@brittlebone.org

CLIC Sargent (Cancer and Leukaemia in Children)
  Horatio House, 77–85 Fulham Palace Road, London W6 8JA
  ☎ 0300 330 0803
  www.clicsargent.org.uk

Children with Cancer
  51 Great Ormond Street, London WC1N 3JQ
  ☎ 0207 404 0808
  ☎ Fax 0207 404 3666
  www.childrenwithcancer.org.uk
  info@childrenwithcancer.org.uk

Scope (Cerebral Palsy)
  6 Market Road, London N7 9PW
  ☎ Helpline 0808 800 3333
  ☎ 0207 619 7100
  www.scope.org.uk
  response@scope.org.uk

Cystic Fibrosis Trust
  11 London Road, Bromley, Kent BR1 1BY
  ☎ Helpline 0300 373 1000
  ☎ 0208 464 7211
  www.cftrust.org.uk
  enquiries@cftrust.org.uk

National Deaf Children's Society
  15 Dufferin Street, London EC1Y 8UR
  ☎ Helpline 0808 800 8800
  ☎ 0207 490 8656 (inc Minicom)
  ☎ Fax 0207 251 5020
  www.ndcs.org.uk
  ndcs@ndcs.org.uk

The Ear Foundation (support for deaf children and young people with cochlear
implants, their families and supporting professionals)
  Marjorie Sherman House, 83 Sherwin Road, Lenton, Nottingham NG7 2FB
  ☎ 01159 821 985
  www.earfoundation.org.uk
  info@earfoundation.org.uk

JDRF (Juvenile Diabetes Research Foundation)
  19 Angel Gate, City Road, London EC1V 2PT
  ☎ 0207 713 2030
  ☎ Fax 0207 713 2031
  www.jdrf.org.uk
  info@jdrf.org.uk

Down's Syndrome Association
  Langdon Down Centre, 2a Langdon Park, Teddington, Middlesex TW11 9PS
  ☎ 03331 212 300
  www.downs-syndrome.org.uk
  info@downs-syndrome.org.uk

British Dyslexia Association
  Unit 8 Bracknell Beeches, Old Bracknell Lane, Bracknell RG12 7BW
  ☎ Helpline 0845 251 9002
  ☎ 0845 251 9003
  ☎ Fax 0845 251 9005
  www.bdadyslexia.org.uk
  helpline@bdadyslexia.org.uk

Dyspraxia Foundation
  8 West Alley, Hitchin, Herts SG5 1EG
  ☎ Helpline 01462 454986
  ☎ 01462 455016
  www.dyspraxiafoundation.org.uk
  dyspraxia@dyspraxiafoundation.org.uk

Epilepsy Action (British Epilepsy Association)
  New Anstey House, Gate Way Drive, Yeadon, Leeds LS19 7XY
  ☎ Helpline 0808 800 5050
  ☎ 0113 210 8800
  ☎ Fax 0113 391 0300
  www.epilepsy.org.uk
  helpline@epilepsy.org.uk

National Eczema Society
  Hill House, Highgate Hill, London N19 5NA
  ☎ Helpline 0800 089 1122
  ☎ 020 7281 3553
  www.eczema.org
  helpline@eczema.org

Mencap *(learning disability)*
  123 Golden Lane, London EC1Y 0RT
  ☎ Helpline 0808 808 1111
  ☎ 020 7454 0454

☎ Fax 020 7608 3254
www.mencap.org.uk
information@mencap.org.uk

Association for All Speech Impaired Children (AFASIC)
20 Bowling Green Lane, London EC1R 0BD
☎ Helpline 0845 355 5577
☎ 0207 490 9410
www.afasicengland.org.uk, www.afasicscotland.org.uk, www.afasiccymru.org.uk

Professional organisations

The Community Practitioners and Health Visitors Association (Unite)
Unite the Union, Unite House, 128 Theobald's Road, Holborn, London
WC1X 8TN
www.unitetheunion.org/cphva

The Royal College of Speech and Language Therapists
2 White Hart Yard, London SE1 1NX
☎ 020 7378 1200
www.rcslt.org
info@rcslt.org

The Chartered Society of Physiotherapy
14 Bedford Row, London WC1R 4ED
☎ 020 7306 6666
www.csp.org.uk

British Association of Occupational Therapists and College of Occupational
Therapists
106–114 Borough High Street, Southwark, London SE1 1LB
☎ 0207 357 6480
www.cot.co.uk
reception@cot.co.uk

The National Portage Association
Kings Court, 17 School Road, Birmingham B28 8JG
☎ 0121 244 1807
☎ Fax 0120 244 1801
www.portage.org.uk
info@portage.org.uk

The Association of Educational Psychologists
4 The Riverside Centre, Frankland Lane, Durham DH1 5TA
☎ 0191 384 9512
☎ Fax 0191 386 5287
www.aep.org.uk

The British Psychological Society
St Andrews House, 48 Princess Road East, Leicester LE1 7DR
☎ 0116 254 9568
☎ Fax 0116 227 1314
www.bps.org.uk
enquiries@bps.org.uk

British Association of Teachers of the Deaf
☎ 0845 643 5181
www.batod.org.uk
exec@batod.org.uk

British Association of Social Workers
16 Kent Street, Birmingham B5 6RD
☎ 0121 622 3911
☎ Fax 0121 622 4860
www.basw.co.uk
online@basw.co.uk

The school, parent and professional SEN team – proforma for contact information

Child's name   Date of birth

Home information

Address

Name of parent/carers

Contact numbers:

    At home

    At work

Other carers:

    Contact number and/or address

Relatives or friends who may be involved

    Name(s)

    Contact details

Language(s) spoken at home

Community language interpreter

    Name

    Contact number

School information

Name of school/early years provision

Address

Telephone number(s)

Name of school/early years keyworker

When available for contact

Name of SENCO

When available for contact

Agreements for home–school communication

Record of information given to parents/carers and how communicated, e.g. special needs policy given in writing and explained in meeting with interpreter

Education support agencies
Name
Contact number

Professionals information

General practitioner:

    Name

    Contact number

Other medical professionals:

    Name

    Role

    Contact number

    Name

    Role

    Contact number

Educational psychologist:

    Name

    Contact number

    When available for contact

Named local authority officer:

    Name

    Contact number

Named person or other parent supporter:

    Name

    Contact number

Other support agencies:

    Name

    Contact number

Social worker:

    Name

    Contact number

    When available for contact

Other information

Special equipment:

    Item(s)

    Provider

    Contact number

    Name of person monitoring use

    Contact number

Any medication:

    Purpose

    Administration details

Inter-agency and parent communication agreement:

    What information will be sent out, to whom and what are the parents' wishes about this

    Any other relevant information given by parents/carers to be communicated to those working within the team

Next annual or other interagency review will be held on

Date form completed

Updated

References

Armstrong, H. B. (2012). Spirited leadership: growing leaders for the future. In S. Roffey (ed.), *Positive Relationships: Evidence Based Practice Across the World*. Dordrecht: Springer.

Baird, G., McConachie, H. & Scrutton, D. (2000). Parents' perceptions of disclosure of the diagnosis of cerebral palsy. *Archives of Disease in Childhood, 83*, 475–80.

Behaviour2learn. (2012). *Personal Communication Passports*. [on-line] available from www.behaviour2learn.co.uk/directory_record/63/personal_communication_passports (accessed 5 March 2013).

Booth, T. & Ainscow, M. (2004). *Index for Inclusion (Early Years and Childcare)*. Bristol: CSIE.

Bromley Council. (2012). *Early Support Programme Leaflet*. London: London Borough of Bromley.

Bronfenbrenner, U. (1979). *The Ecology of Human Development: Experiences by Nature and Design*. Cambridge, MA: Harvard University Press.

Butt, A. & Cosser, C. (2004). Supporting transition: pre school setting into first placement. In M. Blamires & J. Moore, *Support Services and Mainstream Schools: A Guide for Working Together*. London: David Fulton.

Campbell-Hall, V., Coulter, A. & Joyce, L. (2009). *Parental Experience of Services for Disabled Children: Qualitative Research (Phase 2) – Exploring the Findings from the National Survey*. Nottingham: DCSF Publications.

Carter, B., Cummings, J. & Cooper, L. (2005). An exploration of best practice in multi-agency working and the experiences of families of children with complex health needs: what works well and what needs to be done to improve practice for the future? *Journal of Clinical Nursing, 16*, 527–39.

Centre for Studies on Inclusive Education (CSIE). (2011). *UN Convention on the Rights of Persons with Disabilities*. [on-line] available from www.csie.org.uk/inclusion/rights-persons-disabilities.shtml (accessed 15 November 2011).

Charles, M. & Horwarth, J. (2009). Investing in interagency training to safeguard children: an act of faith or an act of reason? *Children & Society, 23*, 364–76.

City of York Council. (2012). *Local Offer: Starting Primary School*. York: City of York Council. [on-line] available from www.yor-ok.org.uk/Starting%20Primary%20School.pdf (accessed 10 June 2013).

Clarke, A. & Statham, J. (2005). Listening to young children: experts in their own lives. *Adoption and Fostering, 29*(1), 45–56.

Clarke, H. & McKay, S. (2008). *Exploring Disability, Family Formation and Break-Up: Reviewing the Evidence*. London: Department for Work and Pensions.

Department for Children, Education, Lifelong Learning and Skills. (2008). *Framework for Children's Learning for 3 to 7 year olds in Wales*. Cardiff: Welsh Assembly Government.

Department for Children, Schools and Families/Department of Health (DCSF/DoH). (2007).

Aiming High for Disabled Children: Better Support for Families. London: Department for Education.

Department for Education (DfE). (2011a). *Support and Aspiration: A New Approach to Special Educational Needs and Disability.* London: Department for Education.

Department for Education (DfE). (2011b). *Independent Review of Early Education and Childcare Qualifications.* [on-line] available from www.education.gov.uk/consultations/index.cfm (accessed 16 November 2011).

Department for Education (DfE). (2011c). *Supporting Families in the Foundation Years.* [on-line] available from https://www.education.gov.uk/publications/standard/publicationDetail/Page1/DFE-01001-2011 (accessed 20 December 2012).

Department for Education (DfE). (2012a). *Support and Aspiration: A New Approach to Special Educational Needs and Disability: Progress and Next Steps.* London: Department for Education.

Department for Education (DfE). (2012b). *Statutory Framework for the Early Years Foundation Stage: Setting the Standards for Learning, Development and Care for Children from Birth to Five.* London: Department for Education.

Department for Education (DfE). (2012c). *Foundations for Quality: Final Report.* [on-line] available from www.education.gov.uk/nutbrownreview (accessed 3 March 2013).

Department for Education (DfE). (2012d). *The 'Core Purpose' of Sure Start Children's Centres.* [on-line] available from www.education.gov.uk/a00191780/core-purpose-of-sure-start-childrens-centres (accessed 19 January 2013).

Department for Education (DfE). (2013). *More Great Childcare.* [on-line] available from https://www.education.gov.uk/publications/eOrderingDownload/More%20Great%20Childcare%20v2.pdf (accessed 1 March 2013).

Department for Education/Department of Health (DfE/DoH). (2011). *Supporting Families in the Foundation Years.* London: Department of Education/Department of Health.

Department for Education and Skills (DfES). (2003). *Every Child Matters.* London: HMSO.

Department for Education and Skills (DfES). (2007). *Statutory Framework for the Early Years Foundation Stage.* London: DfES Publications.

Department of Education (Northern Ireland) (DENI). (2005). *Supplement to the Code of Practice on the Identification and Assessment of Special Educational Needs.* Belfast: Department of Education Northern Ireland.

Department of Education (Northern Ireland) (DENI). (2010). *Early Years (0–6) Strategy: Evidence Based Paper.* Belfast: Department of Education Northern Ireland.

Department of Education (Northern Ireland) (DENI). (2012). *Review of Special Educational Needs and Inclusion.* [on-line] available from www.deni.gov.uk/index/support-and-development-2/special_educational_needs_pg/review_of_special_educational_needs_and_inclusion.htm (accessed 1 March 2013).

Department of Health. (2011). *Health Visitor Implementation Plan 2011–2015: A Call to Action, February 2011.* [on-line] available from www.dh.gov.uk/en/Publicationsandstatistics/Publications/PublicationsPolicyAndGuidance/DH_124202 (accessed 19 January 2013).

Dolan, P. & McGrath, B. (2006). Enhancing support for young people in need: reflections on informal and formal sources of help. In P. Dolan, J. Canavan & J. Pinkerton (eds), *Family Support as Reflective Practice.* London: Jessica Kingsley Publishers.

Dolan, P., Pinkerton, J. & Canavan, J. (2006). Family support: from description to reflection. In P. Dolan, J. Canavan & J. Pinkerton (eds), *Family Support as Reflective Practice.* London: Jessica Kingsley Publishers.

Dowling, E. & Elliott, D. (2012). *Understanding Children's Needs When Parents Separate.* London: Speechmark Press.

Early Support. (2010a). *Background Information: Health Services.* Nottingham: DCSF Publications.

Early Support. (2010b). *Background Information: People You Meet.* Nottingham: DCSF Publications.

Early Support. (2010c). *Background Information: Social Services.* Nottingham: DCSF Publications.

Early Support. (2012). *Key Working: Improving Outcomes For All – Evidence, Provision, Systems and Structures.* [on-line] available from www.ncb.org.uk/media/847692/key_working_position_paper_final_november_2012comp.pdf (accessed 19 January 2013).

Freeman, M. (2007) Why it remains important to take children's rights seriously. *International Journal of Children's Rights, 15,* 5–23.

Getting it right for every child (GIRFEC) in Lanarkshire. (2011). *Toolkit Item 05 Multi Agency Charter.* [on-line] available from www.girfecinlanarkshire.co.uk/2011/06/item-05-multi-agency-charter/ (accessed 20 December 2012).

Greco, V., Sloper, P., Webb, R. & Beecham, J. (2007). Key worker services for disabled children: the views of parents. *Children and Society, 21,* 162–74.

HM Government. (2008). *Information Sharing: Guidance for Practitioners and Managers.* [on-line] available from https://www.education.gov.uk/publications/standard/publicationDetail/Page1/DCSF-00807-2008 (accessed 20 December 2012).

HM Government. (2011). *Early Intervention: The Next Steps.* London: Cabinet Office.

Millar, S. (1995) *Use of Personal Passports with Deafblind People (Final Report).* Edinburgh: Scottish Office Education Department/Scotland SENSE.

Mollard, C. (2003) *Why It's Worth It: Inclusive Education in Scotland – A Parents' Perspective.* Edinburgh: SHS Trust.

Moran, P., Jacobs, C., Bunn, A. & Bifulco, A. (2007). Multi-agency working: implications for an early-intervention social work team. *Child and Family Social Work 2007, 12,* 143–51.

National Autistic Society (NAS). (2013). *Parent to Parent Service.* [on-line] available from www.autism.org.uk/our-services/advice-and-information-services/parent-to-parent-service.aspx (accessed 14 January 2013).

National Children's Bureau/Department for Education (NCB/DfE). (2012). *A Know How Guide: The EYFS Progress Check at Age 2.* [on-line] available from www.ncb.org.uk/ey/peertopeersupport (accessed 2 June 2012).

National Leadership and Innovation Agency for Healthcare (NLIAH). (2007). *Learning to Collaborate: Lessons in Effective Partnership Working in Health and Social Care.* Cardiff: NHS Wales.

Office of the United Nations High Commissioner for Human Rights. (2011). *Convention on the Rights of the Child.* [on-line] available from www2.ohchr.org/english/law/crc.htm (accessed 15 November 2011).

Pemberton, S. & Mason, J. (2008). Co-production and Sure Start children's centres: reflecting upon users' perspectives and implications for service delivery, planning and evaluation. *Social Policy & Society, 8*(1), 13–24.

Read, M. & Rees, M. (2010). Working in teams in early years settings. In C. Cable, L. Miller & G. Goodliff (eds), *Working with Children in the Early Years.* London: Routledge.

Roffey, S. (2002). *School Behaviour and Families: Frameworks for Working Together.* London: David Fulton.

Roffey, S. (2004). The home–school interface for behaviour: a conceptual framework for co-constructing reality. *Educational and Child Psychology, 21*(4), 95–108.

Roffey, S. (2005). *'Respect' in Practice: The Challenge of Emotional Literacy in Education.* [on-line] available from Australian Association for Research in Education http://publications.aare.edu.au/05pap/rof05356.pdf (accessed 11 May 2013).

Roffey, S. (2006). *Circle Time for Emotional Literacy.* London: Sage Publications.

Roffey, S. (ed.) (2012). *Positive Relationships: Evidence Based Practice Across the World.* Dordrecht: Springer.

Roffey, S. (2014). *Circle Solutions for Student Wellbeing*. London: Sage Publications.

Rose, J. (2009). Dilemmas of inter-professional collaboration: can they be resolved? *Children & Society*. [on-line] available from http://onlinelibrary.wiley.com.libezproxy.open.ac.uk/doi/10.1111/j.1099-0860.2009.00268.x/pdf (accessed 6 December 2012).

Rouse, M. (2007). Enhancing effective inclusive practice: knowing, doing and believing. In *Kairaranga*. Wellington: New Zealand Ministry of Education.

Sebba, J. & Sachdev, D. (1997). *What Works in Inclusive Education?* Ilford: Barnado's.

Scope. (2012). *Face2Face: The One to One Befriending Service for Parents of Disabled Children*. [on-line] available from www.scope.org.uk/face2face (accessed 14 January 2013).

Scottish Government. (2009). *The Education (Additional Support for Learning) (Scotland) Acts 2004 & 2009: Consultation on Changes to the Secondary Legislation and Supporting Children's Learning Code of Practice*. [on-line] available from www.scotland.gov.uk/Resource/Doc/290541/0089284.pdf (accessed 15 November 2011).

Scottish Government/COSLA. (2008). *The Early Years Framework*. [on-line] available from www.scotland.gov.uk/Resource/Doc/257007/0076309.pdf (accessed 16 November 2011).

Shannon, D. & Cooper, A. (2013). Draft content re. background to CAN (unpublished paper). Blackpool SEND Team.

Tickell, C. (2011). *The Early Years: Foundations for Health, Life and Learning*. London: HM Government.

Index

Page numbers in *italics* denote tables and case studies.